British Freshwater Fishes

British Freshwater Fishes

Factors Affecting their Distribution

by Margaret E. Varley
M.A., Ph.D.
St Hilda's College, Oxford

Fishing News (Books) Limited
110 Fleet Street, London, E.C.4

A PIONEER
OF FISHERY RESEARCH

Frank Buckland 1826–1880

**This is a Buckland Foundation
Book—one of a series providing
permanent record of annual
lectures maintained by a bequest
of the late Frank Buckland**

Printed by The Whitefriars Press Limited, London and Tonbridge

Contents

Page

Preface 11

Introduction 13

Chapter 1.
The origin of the British freshwater fish fauna . . 19

Chapter 2.
Water temperature and dissolved oxygen as environmental
factors affecting fishes 29

Chapter 3.
The distribution of freshwater fishes in relation to
topography 53

Chapter 4.
The annual climatic cycle and its effect on freshwater
fishes 87

Chapter 5.
The feeding of freshwater fishes 111

Chapter 6.
Commercial aspects of freshwater fishes . . . 131

Bibliography 140

Index 145

List of Plates

Plate		Page
1	The West Dart river above Two Bridges (Devonshire)	65
2	The Afon Elan in central Wales (Radnorshire)	66
3	The River Wye above Rhayader (Radnorshire)	67
4	The River Coln at Bibury (Gloucestershire)	68
5	The River Yarty near Axminster (Devonshire)	69
6	The River Thames at Godstow (Berkshire and Oxfordshire)	70
7	The Great Ouse River at St Neots (Huntingdonshire)	71
8	The River Trent at Swarkeston (Derbyshire)	72
9	Loch Rannoch (Perthshire)	73
10	Loch Tummel (Perthshire)	74
11	Blenheim Lake, Woodstock (Oxfordshire)	75
12	Lochan an Daim (Perthshire)	76
13	The brown trout *Salmo trutta*	77
14	Two views of a female brown trout "cutting a redd" in a shallow aquarium	78
15	"Eyed ova" of the brown trout	79
16	"Alevin" of the brown trout	79
17	Egg of perch, *Perca fluviatilis*, about to hatch	80
18	"Alevin" of perch, immediately after hatching	80
19	An example of a food chain	81
20	Photograph illustrating the feeding of a carnivorous fish	82
21	A group of fish (pike, trout and perch) in an aquarium	83
22	Trout, "char" and perch in an aquarium	84

The illustration on the dust jacket of this book is taken from a photograph kindly supplied by *Angling Times* and shows a section of the R. Lugg, near Hereford.

List of Figures

Figure   *Page*

1   Sketch map of British coastline now and after last ice-age   20

2   Map of British Isles, showing where char and white-fishes are found   22

3   Map of the north Atlantic Ocean to show breeding grounds of freshwater eels and migration routes of their larvae   23

4   Temperature tolerance diagrams for speckled trout, roach and goldfish   31

5   Histograms to show lethal temperatures for brown trout acclimatized to different temperatures   34

6   Hypothetical curves illustrating the relationship between basal metabolism, activity, maintenance requirement and temperature   36

7   Diagrams showing annual changes in temperature and dissolved oxygen in deep and shallow lakes   40

8   Relation of standard metabolism to temperature in different species of fish   45

9   Histograms showing relationship between oxygen requirements and temperature for four species of fish   47

10   Showing relationship between temperature and metabolism for brown and speckled trouts   48

11   Diagram illustrating relation between fish zones and gradient and width of flowing waters   56

12   Outlines and sections of various fishes, illustrating different habits of life   58

Figure   *Page*

13   Sections through the trout and bream zones of rivers, showing difference in substratum, vegetation and dissolved oxygen in summer   59

14   Sections of three types of lake showing differences in substratum, in vegetation and in dissolved oxygen conditions in summer   61

15   Diagram showing breeding seasons of British freshwater fishes, with special reference to annual changes of daylight and water temperature   89

16   Showing that spawning time of speckled trout can be altered by using artificial light   92

17   Comparative survival rates of brown trout fry in screened reaches of a stream   99

18   Mortality of powan eggs in Loch Lomond   101

19   Illustrating the relationship between sexual maturity, size and age in fishes   103

20   Showing different types of life history found among British freshwater fishes   106

21   A food web, with arrows indicating the directions of energy flow   112

22   Comparison of guts of salmon (carnivorous) and roach (omnivorous)   116

23   Pharyngeal teeth of seven species of cyprinids   117

24   Carp with mouth closed and open   117

25   The depth of penetration into the bottom by feeding fishes   118

Preface

The three Buckland Lectures for 1963 were given in Glasgow, Leeds and Nottingham and I would like to thank Professor C. M. Yonge, Professor J. M. Dodd and Professor E. J. W. Barrington for their kindness in acting as Chairmen. Each lecture has been divided into two chapters in this book. The material in the Introduction formed a necessary part of all three lectures.

My special thanks are due to my friends Dr Rosemary McConnell and Dr Winifred Frost who read through the MS and with whom I have had many valuable discussions about fishes over many years. Any mistakes or mis-statements are, however, my sole responsibility. I must also record my gratitude to my husband who first introduced me to animal ecology and who has shown great forbearance while I prepared these lectures and this book.

M. E. V.

Introduction

Francis Trevelyan Buckland was a great naturalist with wide interests in the best Victorian tradition. As Inspector of Fisheries for England and Wales he became concerned about economic aspects of fish, and the Lecturers sponsored by his Foundation are required "to pay all possible attention to the subject of Economic Fish Culture".

Some of our freshwater fishes have an economic value as food, notably salmon and trout and to a lesser extent eels. The real value of most of our fishes is, however, recreational – the provision of the raw materials for angling. It is difficult to say exactly how many anglers there are in the British Isles; the Editor of "Where to fish 1963–1964" estimates that there are $2\frac{1}{2}$ million, which is about 1 person in 25 and more than the numbers who watch football matches. The popularity of the sport is increasing. Most of these anglers fish in local waters most of the time but may go elsewhere for holiday fishing. They spend a lot of money on equipment and on groundbait. They are an important element in the community interested in resisting the spread of water pollution and water abstraction and wishing to preserve the purity of rivers and some of the peace and beauty of the countryside.

Anglers are often divided into "game" and "coarse" fishermen but many of the latter now take an interest in trout fishing, part of the province of the former. Perhaps the most striking difference between the two is that the coarse fisherman nearly always returns his fish to the water, as he hopes, undamaged, whereas the game fisherman wishes to return home with something to eat although, of course, he may accept size and bag limits on many waters. This is sometimes presented as a major difference in outlook – with the coarse fisherman being more interested in pure sport than the game fisherman – but I suspect that the tradition has much to do with the relative edibility of the fishes caught, and certainly the coarse fishes are better adapted to survive imprisonment in a keep-net than are the salmonids.

Coarse fishing usually includes the liberal use of groundbait, for the angler must attract and hold a shoal of fishes in his " swim" and he must adjust his bait and his tackle to the species he really wants to catch. Some species present a tremendous challenge and require highly sophisticated techniques. The game fisherman does not use groundbait and is by tradition restricted to special techniques such as "wet" and "dry fly" fishing. He seeks to locate a fish in its "lie" and then to take the fish by casting to it, and his success often depends on divining what the fish are eating and using the appropriate lure, usually an artificial fly. I suspect that some of the traditions of the game fisherman are designed to make it more difficult to catch trout, since these fish will feed greedily on groundbait and are often eager to take the maggot or worm meant for other species. Whatever their type of fishing, however, all anglers must participate actively in their sport and all good anglers must study their prey and the waters in which they live, so that they can plan their tactics efficiently.

Since methods of fishing vary with the species to be captured, anglers want to know what sort of fish to expect in a water; so they should be interested in the factors that govern the distribution of fishes in British fresh waters. Why are the fishes in a canal different from those in a moorland stream? Certain types of angling are preferred to others and enthusiasts wish to spread their favourite species by introducing them elsewhere; how likely are such introductions to be successful and what consequences may follow? These are some of the questions I asked myself when preparing these lectures. The survival of a species of animal in a given environment depends on two major factors: firstly, its own physiological potentialities and limitations, and secondly, the competition to which it is subjected by other species. As a physiologist, I can feel justified in talking about the ranges of tolerance of fishes; and fresh waters, with their wide range of variation in physical and chemical conditions, present a very favourable environment for the study of possible correlations between physiological adaptability and actual distribution. I shall also consider competition between species, as implied by their feeding and breeding habits.

The British freshwater fishes belong to two zoological groups. The lampreys are descendants of very primitive vertebrates which do not have true jaws. There are three species and they are fairly widespread in clean rivers; their flesh was highly esteemed in the Middle Ages. I shall say nothing more about them. The sturgeon and sterlet, which are still caught occasionally in our rivers, are primitive bony fishes. All the rest are more advanced bony fishes and belong to the super-order *Teleostei*, which includes 95 per cent of all fishes living today. There are more than 20,000 species, with an immense range of morphological and physiological adaptations; most of these species are marine, and the origin of the Teleost fishes was probably in the sea during the Cretaceous period some 70 million years ago.

Our common freshwater fishes belong to a small number of orders of Teleosts (see Table 1). The Clupeiformes are the most primitive order and include many marine fishes. The Cypriniformes are closely related to them but all members of this order have a series of little bones, called Weber's ossicles, between the swimbladder and the inner ear. This is the most successful of all Teleost orders in fresh waters, with a world-wide distribution. The eels belong to a small peculiar order, probably derived from Clupeiformes. The perch, ruffe and bullhead are freshwater representatives of a Teleost order which is structurally very advanced and extremely successful in the sea. The systematic position of the stickleback is controversial. The burbot is a member of another rather peculiar order which is of great economic importance because it includes many marine fishes used as food, e.g. cod.

A few marine fishes may live in estuaries and move up rivers into fresh water. Grey mullet, flounders and shads are fairly common in some rivers in the lower reaches, but I shall not discuss them further because I consider them to be basically marine in habit.

TABLE 1. THE SYSTEMATIC POSITION OF BRITISH FRESHWATER
FISHES

Class Cyclostomata
　　Lampreys (*Lampetra planeri, Lampetra fluviatilis, Petromyzon marinus*)
Class Osteichthyes
　Superorder Chondrostei
　　　　　Sturgeon (*Acipenser sturio*), sterlet (*Acipenser ruthenus*).
　Superorder Teleostei
　　Order Clupeiformes (formerly Isospondyli)
　　　suborder Salmonoidei: Salmon (*Salmo salar*), brown and sea trout (*Salmo trutta*), whitefish (*Coregonus spp.*), char (*Salvelinus alpinus*), grayling (*Thymallus thymallus*).
　　　　[Rainbow trout (*Salmo gairdnerii*), speckled trout (*Salvelinus fontinalis*)].
　　　suborder Esocoidei: Pike (*Esox lucius*).

　　Order Cypriniformes (formerly Ostariophysi)
　　　suborder Cyprinoidei: Bream (*Abramis brama*), white or silver bream (*Blicca bjoernka*), bleak (*Alburnus alburnus*), barbel (*Barbus barbus*), carp (*Cyprinus carpio*), crucian carp (*Carassius carassius*), goldfish (*Carassius auratus*), gudgeon (*Gobio gobio*), roach (*Rutilus rutilus*), rudd (*Scardinius erythrophthalmus*), dace (*Leuciscus leuciscus*), chub (*Squalius cephalus*), tench (*Tinca tinca*), minnow (*Phoxinus phoxinus*), stone loach (*Nemacheilus barbatulus*), spiny loach (*Cobitis taenia*).
　　　　[Bitterling (*Rhodeus amarus*), ide or orfe (*Idus idus*)].
　　　suborder Siluroidei: [Catfish or wels (*Siluris glanis*)].

　　Order Apodes: Eel (*Anguilla anguilla*).
　　Order Gadiformes: Burbot (*Lota lota*).
　　Order Gasterosteiformes: Three-spined stickleback (*Gasterosteus aculeatus*), ten-spined stickleback (*Pygosteus pungitius*).
　　Order Perciformes.
　　　suborder Percoidei: Ruffe (*Acerina cernua*), perch (*Perca fluviatilis*).
　　　　[Pikeperch (*Lucioperca lucioperca*)].
　　　suborder Cottoidei: Bullhead or miller's thumb (*Cottus gobio*).

Shads (Clupeiformes), flounders (Pleuronectiformes) and grey mullet (Mugiliformes) also enter rivers but are basically marine or estuarine fishes.

[] Species introduced in the last 100 years are given in square brackets.

The majority of our fish species thus belong to the orders Clupeiformes and Cypriniformes and particularly to the suborders Salmonoidei and Cyprinoidei. Most of the discussion which follows will be concerned with members of these two suborders and the differences between them and among them.

Chapter 1

The origin of the British freshwater fish fauna

THE present distribution of animals depends on the range of tolerance of each species and also on its past history. Each new species evolves in a definite area and may then spread away from this. The speed with which it spreads and the area it eventually occupies depend on its means of dispersal and how effective this is in the circumstances prevailing at the time. Geological changes and climatic fluctuations may lead to wholesale changes in the fauna and these have been of great importance in the case of our own freshwater fishes.

For freshwater fishes, as for many terrestrial groups of animals, the British fauna is poor compared with that of continental Europe—which is itself poor compared with North America. Such common continental fish as the orfe are found only in ornamental ponds and until recently we have lacked the little bitterling, *Rhodeus amarus*, quite common on the other side of the English Channel. Our small loaches are unimpressive compared with the large catfish or wels of the Danube, *Siluris glanis*, also recently introduced here. The main reason for our limited fauna is that the glaciations during the Pleistocene Era virtually eliminated the fauna which had been living in Britain; the retreat of the ice was followed by colonization from the Continent.

Before the Ice Age, perhaps one million years ago, the British Isles were joined with the continent of Europe; much of the North Sea was land and the Thames was a tributary of the Rhine which flowed across "Doggerland" into the restricted North Sea (see Figure 1). Conditions on land were temperate and the fauna included the amphibious hippopotamus. There were probably four major glaciations, with recessions and periods of warmer climate between them. The ice sheet came furthest south during the second glaciation and covered the whole country north of a line along the Thames valley and

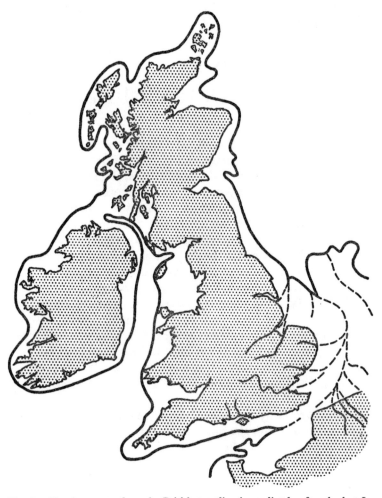

Fig. 1.—Sketch map to show the British coastline immediately after the last Ice Age. Present land area stippled; broken lines show ancient rivers over "Dogger-land".

across to Gloucester. Probably the greater part of Ireland was also glaciated. The unglaciated part of southern England and south-western Ireland must have been very cold and it is likely that almost the whole of the fish fauna was destroyed.

After the final retreat of the ice sheets, the climate gradually became warmer and the land first became tundra, then steppe and then forest. Pollen analysis has revealed that birch (the first of the trees) gradually disappeared and pine became dominant and then this was joined by hazel and eventually replaced by deciduous forest, at first mainly elm, then oak and later alder mixed with oak. The appearance of alder at the end of the Boreal period indicates that the climate became warmer and more equable, and this may have been the result of the breaking of the Channel land bridge and the establishment of sea circulation all round Britain. Changes in land level resulted in more or less the conditions we map today. There is still some argument about the timing of the various events but the ice probably began to retreat about 15,000 B.C. and the Straits of Dover were probably formed about 7,000 B.C., about 2,000 years after Britain became forested with pine and hazel and some elm and oak trees. At this time, Ireland was still joined to Scotland via north-eastern Donegal, Islay and Jura but this link broke a few thousand years later.

It is possible that our southern rivers contained chars and whitefishes during the glaciation, for these live in Greenland, Iceland, Scandinavia and Siberia today. It is likely that these fishes were anadromous, spawning in the rivers but migrating downstream into the sea and feeding there, as do the salmon and sea-trout. In Iceland the char still has this habit, whereas our char and our whitefish (except the houting) are all confined to deep, rocky lakes and spend their whole lives in fresh water (see Figure 2). As the ice retreated, these salmonid fishes would be able to colonize more northerly rivers by moving along the coasts. Eventually they must have lost the anadromous habit and became resident in the lakes where we find them today. This change in habit occurred sufficiently long ago for our char to have differentiated morphologically to an extent which persuaded Tate Regan (1911) that there were fifteen separate species. Opinion on such questions has recently been modified and many experts today include these all as varieties of the alpine char, *Salvelinus alpinus*. There are perhaps nine British species of whitefish, genus *Coregonus*, one of which, the rare houting, *C. oxyrhynchus*, is anadromous and also found in the Rhine while the rest are confined to certain lakes; some of these are probably varieties of Continental species of *Coregonus*.

As the climate mellowed, other fish species colonized

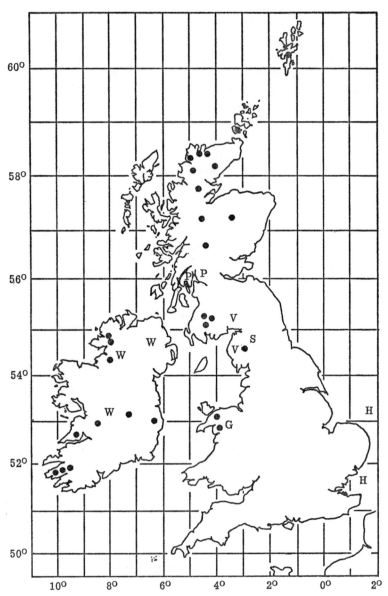

Fig. 2.—Map of the British Isles to show the areas where char and whitefishes are found today. ●, char; W, pollan; V, vendace; S, schelly; G, gwyniad; P, pouting; H, houting.

Britain. There were two routes by which they could arrive: either via the sea or else via river basins. While the Thames formed part of the Rhine, fishes from the latter could move into the former; they could occasionally cross the watershed from this basin into neighbouring drainage areas and thus spread across country from a focus in the south-east of England.

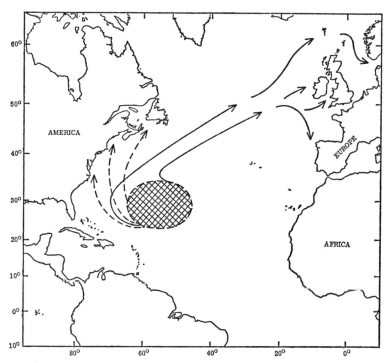

Fig. 3.—Sketch map to show breeding grounds of the eels in the Sargasso Sea (cross-hatched area) and drift of the *leptocephalus* larvae of American eels (broken lines) and European eels (full lines). [*After Colman, 1950*]

Much later the construction of canals would simplify the passage across watersheds. The latest time at which fish could move into England without negotiating the sea would be just before the Channel land bridge was broken, about 9,000 years ago, and the interval between the climate warming up and the disappearance of this bridge is only a few thousand years.

Fishes able to travel through the sea can achieve a wide dispersal rapidly since in theory they can enter any river where conditions are suitable. Most of our freshwater fishes cannot survive in salt water; those which can are the eel, the sticklebacks and the salmonids (trout, salmon, etc.).

The eel is catadromous; it breeds in the sea but spends many years feeding in fresh waters. Eels are distributed passively, as *leptocephalus* larvae, by the ocean currents; after hatching in the Sargasso Sea, they are carried across the Atlantic by the Gulf Stream. They metamorphose when they reach the continental shelf of Europe and then swim up the nearest rivers. Because of our position in relation to the ocean currents, many elvers attempt to swim up our rivers, especially those on the west coast (Figure 3).

Sticklebacks move downstream and into salt water for the winter, returning to fresh water in the spring; they are not strong swimmers and might be expected to move rather slowly from one river to another. The salmonids, however, are good swimmers and have in fact succeeded in colonizing all rivers available to them. Since salmonid fishes typically "home" to spawn in the river where they lived as fry, the colonization of new rivers must have been a fairly unusual event; but when eggs did develop in a new river, fish from them would have the instinct to breed in that place themselves and so the population would establish itself if other circumstances permitted. Impassable falls are natural barriers and polluted estuaries are more modern barriers to the passage of migratory fish.

Brown trout are a variety of sea-trout which stopped moving down to the sea; many of them move into lakes or down rivers as they grow older and then ascend to the upper tributaries to spawn. As a result of colonization from the sea and then the reduction of the migratory habit, there are now brown trout on remote islands, for instance, the Outer Hebrides, where there are no other species of completely freshwater fishes. During the Ice Age there were probably sea-trout in the Mediterranean Sea, but now there are none, although brown trout live in many rivers flowing into this sea. Here the species *Salmo trutta* has shown a similar change in habit to that suggested for *Salvelinus alpinus* in the British Isles. Both species are represented only by freshwater races at the southern limit of their distribution but include anadromous races further north.

There are a few freshwater forms of the salmon, *Salmo salar*, in North America but this fish does not seem to lose the migratory habit as easily as trout and char. When brown trout from Britain are transplanted to other parts of the world, their descendants sometimes become anadromous; this has happened in Canada, New Zealand and the Falkland Islands.

Some species of lampreys and sturgeons also are anadromous so they, too, could have colonized our rivers from the sea but the rest of our native fauna must have entered overland and via the river systems after the Ice Age. Most of these fishes are common in the south-east of England and become less common away from this centre of distribution. Thus the white bream is found in rivers in eastern England from the Thames north to Yorkshire, and the barbel is found "only in . . . affluents of the prehistoric Rhine" (Magri MacMahon, 1946), i.e. in the Thames and the Trent and a few others; the burbot is found only in east coast rivers from Suffolk to Durham; the bream and chub have got a little further but are absent from West Wales, south-west England and most of Scotland; the gudgeon is not found in Scotland, the Lake District, Wales or Cornwall; even the roach is not found in north Scotland and is local in Devon, Cornwall and the Lake District.

These areas of distribution are believed to be the result of the natural dispersal of these fishes but men have transplanted fishes in earlier centuries as they do now, probably first for food and later, as now, for sport. Perch and pike were greatly esteemed as food in the Middle Ages and were probably the fish kept in their ponds by medieval monks. They now have an almost universal distribution where waters are suitable. Carp were introduced later – Izaak Walton quotes the rhyme:

> *Hops and turkies, carps and beer,*
> *Came into England all in a year*

and suggests that this was about one century before he wrote "The Compleat Angler" in 1653. The carp is really a native of China and Central Asia but has been spread as a pondfish for food.

Ireland remained connected to Scotland after the Channel Bridge broke but this connection must have disappeared before the fishes colonizing Britain via the Channel Bridge had reached

Scotland. There is good reason to believe that only migratory fishes colonized Ireland by their own efforts and all others have been introduced by man. Barbel, chub, bleak, ruffe, bullhead and grayling are all still absent from that country, and 90 per cent of the introduced fishes are found in the Shannon and Erne river systems. Perch, rudd and pike are the most common of these fishes but there are also many bream locally and occasionally tench, which are being encouraged by the Inland Fisheries Trust. Carp are being kept carefully to enclosed waters without access to rivers. The River Blackwater flowing through County Cork was a salmon and trout river with pike also there in the 1890s, but dace and roach were released and have now spread through the system to the extent that in some reaches fly-fishing will yield only dace – to the dismay of devoted trout fishermen.

A few fishes have somewhat odd distributions such as the tench, which is very irregularly dispersed but absent from north Scotland, and the rudd, also with a haphazard distribution but common in the Broads, the Cam and the Great Ouse; this fish is widespread in Ireland where it is often called "roach". The grayling has a very local distribution but has lately been introduced into a number of rivers.

Permission for the import of freshwater fishes from abroad must now be obtained from the Ministry of Agriculture, Fisheries and Food, and this acts as a check to enthusiasts who would like to introduce for instance the American large-mouth and small-mouth bass. The late Duke of Bedford imported some European fishes such as wels and pikeperch into ponds at Woburn but these have spread only to a very limited extent, if at all. Pikeperch, a fish much esteemed in central and northern Europe, has been introduced recently again into ponds isolated from any river system. The bitterling is said now to be naturalized in Yorkshire. Very recently, the Ministry has started rearing Chinese grass carp, *Ctenopharyngodon* in the Fens in the hope of controlling water weeds.

The situation about movements within the country seems somewhat chaotic. Many River Boards take an interest in angling and do their best to control the movement of fishes within their areas; others are less enlightened and some fishing clubs indulge in considerable moving of fishes. An up-to-date map of the present distribution would be of great interest and I hope this may soon be organized.

The import of species new to our fauna may seem attractive but needs very careful thought. The existing species in their natural habitats probably form balanced communities and the balance is easily upset, with results that are not easy to predict. Carp introduced into South Africa and into North America have done a great deal of damage to the native fish faunas because of their habit of stirring up the bottom mud. A voracious predatory fish like the wels might be a considerable nuisance if it escaped from ponds into neighbouring river systems. The introduction of fish from northern Europe is likely to be the least objectionable course, since our fauna is an attenuated version of the north European fish fauna and the study of communities there gives a good idea of how the balance here might change. Fish from entirely distinct faunas are potentially much more dangerous. There is also the chance of introducing diseases or parasites with the fishes and this is the official reason for the control of imports by the Ministry.

The rainbow trout, *Salmo gairdnerii*, is a foreign species which was introduced as a sporting fish about 80 years ago. This species is native to North American rivers draining into the Pacific Ocean where it occupies the same niche as our brown trout, *Salmo trutta*, in European rivers. Some varieties (e.g. steelheads) are migratory and the breeding season varies from November to March according to variety. The rainbow trout grows slightly faster than the brown trout under identical conditions and it is more hardy since it can withstand higher temperatures and lower oxygen concentrations. When mixed groups are grown together in aquaria, the rainbow fry are more aggressive than the brown trout fry and the latter grow slowly and many die. Rainbows were planted in American rivers draining into the Atlantic Ocean and the first successful introductions into Europe were probably to England in 1884 and to Germany in 1886. Although widely distributed here, the species has only become established as a breeding population in Blagdon Reservoir, the Derbyshire Wye and a few other small waters (Worthington, 1940, 1941); elsewhere populations are maintained entirely by stocking with fish reared in hatcheries. Thus this fish has not driven out our native trout and seems unable to breed successfully in most of our waters. Perhaps this is because the native brown trout spawn earlier, so that their fry begin to feed earlier and become large enough to dominate and starve the rainbow fry when these emerge from the gravel later in the spring. The rainbow trout is, however, a better pond fish and is cultivated for the table in Denmark; there are now some rainbow trout farms in the British Isles, too.

Another salmonid, the speckled trout, *Salvelinus fontinalis*, has also been introduced from North America where it lives in the cooler rivers draining into the Atlantic Ocean. This relation of our char is very like the brown trout in habits and physiology but it has not been successful here. Attempts to introduce the huchen, a large salmonid from the Danube, into the Thames as a substitute for our salmon failed completely. All these salmonids were potentially very desirable fish both for their sporting qualities and because they are good to eat. Yet another strange salmonid has lately been captured occasionally in British estuaries, the humpback or pink salmon, *Oncorhynchus gorbuscha*. This is the result of Russian efforts to introduce this Pacific species into rivers flowing into the Barents Sea. The habits of this fish are so different from those of *Salmo salar* that competition between them is extremely unlikely.

Thus, some knowledge of history during the last ten thousand years is necessary to understand the distribution of our freshwater fishes today. So far, however, I have been discussing river systems and drainage basins but within these the species are not randomly distributed by any means. Trout, minnows and dace are characteristic of rapidly flowing water, though the first two also live in lakes; tench and bream are characteristic of deep, slow or stagnant and muddy water. To understand why different types of water have different fish faunas, we must consider the fishes' physiology and behaviour in detail and attempt to define their ranges of tolerance and relate these to the physical, chemical and biological conditions in various waters.

Chapter 2

Water temperature and dissolved oxygen as environmental factors affecting fishes

THE Ice Age greatly limited our freshwater fauna and flora and it is evident that water temperature is one of the most important factors affecting freshwater organisms, including fishes. These are all cold-blooded organisms (poikilotherms) which means that their body temperature varies with the external temperature. A very actively swimming fish may be warmer than the water round it, but as soon as it stops swimming it will cool down.

Most chemical reactions are affected by temperature and proceed more rapidly at higher temperatures. The processes of life are basically chemical reactions in which organic substances are either built up into the complex proteins and other compounds of which bodies are made, or else are broken down for the production of energy which is used for movement and for the other vital bodily activities. Many of these chemical reactions are controlled by enzymes, themselves complex proteins, which act like catalysts in simple chemical reactions. Proteins become denatured at high temperatures usually below 60°C and this sets an upper limit to the temperatures at which life is possible. The formation of ice crystals in living cells destroys vital structures, but animals can survive below the freezing point of water because their body fluids contain salts and therefore freeze at temperatures lower than 0°C, just as sea water freezes at lower temperatures than fresh water. However, 0°C sets an approximate lower limit to the survival of freshwater fishes.

Thus, in theory, there is a possibility of fishes surviving over a range of water temperatures between freezing point (0°C) and the temperature of denaturation of proteins. Species with a tolerance for a big range of temperatures are called eurytherms and the most eurythermal fish species so far described is the goldfish (*Carassius auratus*) which can survive between 0°C and 41°C. Most of our fishes are more restricted in their thermal range and some (stenotherms) are very restricted.

At low temperatures, chemical reactions proceed slowly and such processes as digestion therefore take a longer time than at higher temperatures. The time taken to react to stimuli may be long, so that the animal is sluggish and cannot obtain very much food. It may survive in a state of almost suspended animation for long periods of time; this state is characteristic of "overwintering" fish, which retreat to concealed places where they rest without feeding through the winter. At the opposite extreme, near the upper lethal temperature, the fish's metabolism is at a very high level so that it may be burning up its food reserves. Digestion is very rapid, but it may not be possible for the fish to obtain and eat sufficient food to supply the requirements of its basal metabolism plus the energy used for movements – and usually it is very active at these temperatures. It may survive for several weeks at such a temperature but waste away during this time and die as a result. At a slightly higher temperature, the fish usually goes through a series of characteristic changes in colour and behaviour. These include bursts of restless swimming alternating with periods when it floats motionless on its side or upside down. The muscles used in swimming seem to be the first to stop functioning and the fish may go on breathing for a little while until the muscles moving the breathing apparatus also stop functioning. The heart is usually still beating at this stage, but erratically, and soon it stops and the fish is dead. The fish often recovers if it is transferred to cooler well-oxygenated water while it is still breathing. Sudden transfer to temperatures above the lethal level results in very rapid death after a short series of convulsive movements. Probably death at the upper lethal temperature is the result of failure of the oxygen supply to the muscles.

Fishes can tolerate sudden changes in temperature, both increases and decreases, within certain limits. When the temperature is raised or lowered gradually, some acclimatization ("acclimation" in Canada and U.S.A.) occurs, provided that the rate of change is sufficiently slow. There is, however, for each species an ultimate upper and ultimate lower lethal temperature, and no amount of acclimatization can alter these. It is possible to construct for each species of fish a diagram

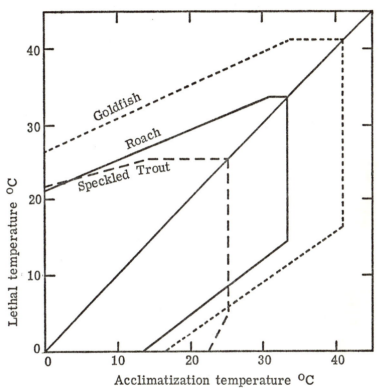

Fig. 4.—Temperature tolerance diagram for the speckled trout, roach and goldfish. The diagonal lines show the upper and lower lethal temperatures for fish acclimatized to different temperatures. The vertical lines at the right-hand side of the diagram show the ultimate upper lethal temperatures for each species. [*Drawn from data from Fry, Hart and Walker (1946), Cocking (1959b) and Fry, Brett ᴸ ᵈd Clawson (1942)*]

showing the relation between the acclimatization temperature and the upper and lower lethal temperatures through its temperature range. Figure 4 shows such diagrams for the speckled trout (a fish related to our char), the roach and the goldfish (a relation of the carp). These three differ in their

temperature relations, the goldfish being eurythermal, the
trout stenothermal and the roach an intermediate type.
Raising the acclimatization temperature by 3°C increases the
upper lethal temperature by 1°C for roach and goldfish over
much of their range, but a 7°C increase in acclimatization
temperature is necessary to raise the upper lethal temperature
of speckled trout by 1°C, and above 15°C no further adjustment
occurs. About 24 hours is necessary for complete acclimatization for each 1°C rise in temperature. The areas enclosed by
these diagrams have been called "areas of tolerance" by Fry
and his collaborators in Canada (Fry *et al.*, 1942). The eurythermal goldfish has an area of tolerance of 1220 units, the
roach 770 units and the stenothermal speckled trout only 625
units. The most stenothermal fish so far described is the pink
or humpback salmon *Oncorhynchus gorbuscha*, with an area of
tolerance of 450 units and an ultimate upper lethal temperature
of 24°C.

One complication in defining lethal temperatures is that
fish can tolerate for a short time a higher temperature than
one which is lethal over a longer period. Individuals of a species
also vary in their resistance and it is usual to test a group of
fish and use the median time of survival (the time taken for
half the fish to die) or find the temperature at which half the
group will survive for 48 hours or 7 days or however long a
convenient test period may be. Figure 5 shows how the upper
lethal temperature for brown trout varies according to temperature of acclimatization and period of observation. Where fish
are subjected to varying temperatures the effects are additive
unless the fish spend several hours at fairly low temperatures
between exposures to high ones.

Upper lethal temperatures for various freshwater fishes are
given in Table 2. It is difficult to compare these because the
conditions of the test are not always described fully. The starred
figures are certainly lower than the ultimate upper lethal
temperatures for those species, because the acclimatization
temperatures were low. Probably it is justifiable to distinguish
three groups:—

1. Fish with upper lethal limits below 28°C, e.g. freshwater
   salmonids (trout, grayling); these are stenotherms.

TABLE 2. UPPER LETHAL TEMPERATURES OF VARIOUS SPECIES
OF FISHES (VARIOUS SOURCES)

Scientific name	Common name	Temperature (°C)
Alevins and young fry of Salmo salar and trutta	Early stages of salmon and trout	23**, 23*
Oncorhynchus gorbuscha	pink salmon	24
Thymallus thymallus	grayling	24·1**
Salvelinus fontinalis	speckled trout	25·3
Salmo trutta	brown trout	26·5
Esox lucius	pike	29
Gobio gobio	gudgeon	29·6*
Acerina cernua	ruffe	30·7*
Abramis brama	bream	31·8*
Scardinius erythrophthalmus	rudd	32·5*
Perca fluviatilis	perch	32·8
Salmo salar	Atlantic salmon	32–34
Rutilus rutilus	roach	33·5
Tinca tinca	tench	35·2
Cyprinus carpio	carp	37
Carassius carassius	crucian carp	39
Carassius auratus	goldfish	41
Cyprinodon macularius	desert pupfish (from Colorado River basin)	52

* acclimatized at 20°C ⎱ The ultimate upper lethal temperatures
⎰ are almost certainly higher than the
** acclimatized at 6°C ⎰ values quoted.

2. Fish with upper lethal limits between 28 and 34°C, e.g. pike, perch, ruffe, roach, gudgeon and the migratory salmon.
3. Fish with upper lethal limits above 34°C, e.g. carp, tench and probably rudd and bream; these are eurytherms.

Fish are sensitive to water temperature and when put in temperature gradients they show definite preferences, depending on their previous thermal experience. They swim away from very high temperatures and usually seek a temperature close to that at which they have been living. After several days in a gradient, they choose temperatures which seem to be characteristic for the species. Thus the rainbow trout chooses

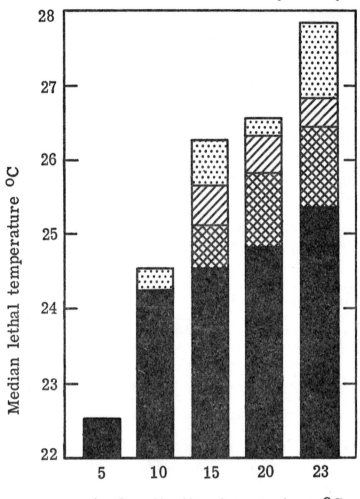

Fig. 5.—Histograms to show the highest temperatures at which half the brown trout in the tested group survived for 7 days (black), 48 hours (cross-stripes), 24 hours (stripes) and 12 hours (dots), after acclimatization at different water temperatures. [*Drawn from data from Gibson, 1951*]

13·6°C, the speckled trout 15°C, the tench 20°C or more, the goldfish 27°C and the carp 32°C. Alabaster (1963) used a channel with a temperature gradient which could be altered and found that the large fish avoided high temperatures but

TABLE 3. TEMPERATURES (IN °C) RECORDED IN THE RIVER TEST
AT LAVERSTOKE (FROM MR. CHARLES SMITH)

	Average maximum	*Average minimum*	*Daily variation*
1959			
October	11	9	0 to 4
November	8·5	7·2	0 to 4·5
December	7·8	6·7	0 to 2·8
1960			
January	7·5	6·1	0·6 to 3·5
February	8	6·4	0·6 to 3·5
March	9·4	7·8	0·6 to 4
April	11	8·5	0·6 to 5
May	13	10·6	0 to 4·5
June	17·8	12·8	3·5 to 7·5
July	15·3	12·5	0 to 4·5
August	14·7	12·5	1 to 4·5
September	13·9	12·5	0 to 3·5

Highest recorded temperature: 19·5°C on June 21 to 23
Lowest recorded temperature: 2·2°C on January 15

large Midland rivers in the summers of 1958 and 1959. The
latter year was hot and dry and many rivers reached record
low levels, but even so the mean temperatures of the Rivers
Trent and Great Ouse were only 21·5°C and the highest
recorded temperature was 25·5°C at Castle Donington on the
Trent. The maximum daily range of all the rivers observed
varied from 1·7 to 2·8°C. When power stations are discharging
hot water from their cooling systems into a river this may
increase the water temperature below their outfall by as much
as 10°C and there may be large diurnal fluctuations, with a
rapid rise as the station begins to generate electricity to cater
for the peak demand. Thus, below power stations, water
temperatures may sometimes rise to 30°C in July and August.

In ponds and lakes, the upper layers of water are warmed
by the sun in spring and summer and this warm "epilimnion"
floats on top of the cool water of the hypolimnion, with a zone
(the thermocline) between them where the temperature
changes suddenly. These warm and cold layers usually remain

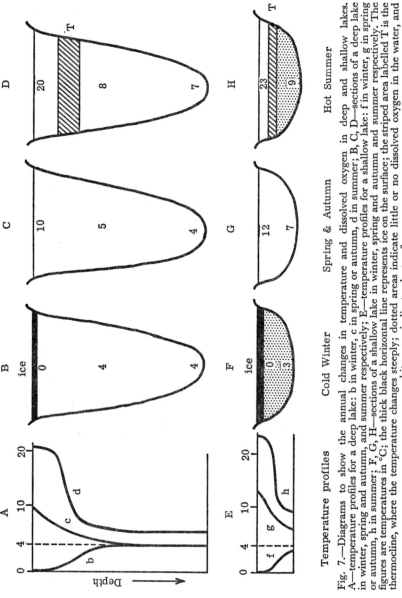

Fig. 7.—Diagrams to show the annual changes in temperature and dissolved oxygen in deep and shallow lakes. A—temperature profiles for a deep lake: b in winter, c in spring or autumn, d in summer; B, C, D—sections of a deep lake in winter, spring and autumn, and summer respectively; E—temperature profiles for a shallow lake: f in winter, g in spring or autumn, h in summer; F, G, H—sections of a shallow lake in winter, spring and autumn and summer respectively. The figures are temperatures in °C; the thick black horizontal line represents ice on the surface; the striped area labelled T is the thermocline, where the temperature changes steeply; dotted areas indicate little or no dissolved oxygen in the water, and white areas indicate plenty of oxygen.

separate through the summer but the epilimnion cools in the autumn and strong winds cause an "overturn" so that the whole body of water assumes the same temperature (see Figure 7). In a cold winter the temperature at the surface may fall below 4°C and an upper layer of cold water, whose surface may freeze, will then float on top of water at 4°C. Shallow water warms and cools faster than deep water and very shallow lakes or ponds may warm up entirely in summer and freeze solid in winter, but most of our standing waters are sufficiently deep to stratify in summer and never freeze completely. The epilimnion of a south-country reservoir may reach more than 20°C in summer but the hypolimnion will then be about 12°C or less; in winter the bottom temperature will probably remain at 4°C when the surface freezes. In productive lakes, especially if they are shallow, the hypolimnion may contain little or no oxygen during the summer but deep lakes, especially if they are not very productive, retain plenty of dissolved oxygen in the cool hypolimnion throughout the year.

In general, it is probable that the natural maximum and minimum temperatures of flowing and standing waters will not be very different from air temperatures. The climatic records listed in Table 4 show that our climate is most equable along the Atlantic coasts and has the greatest annual range in the English Midlands. Summer temperatures rarely rise much above 20°C and winter temperatures rarely fall to zero. The climate of mountains is, of course, very different and climatic conditions at Moor House, on the upper Tees, have been compared by Manley (1936) to those of southern Iceland.

Are any of our freshwater fishes limited in their distribution by temperature alone? Our char (*Salvelinus alpinus*) and whitefish (*Coregonus* spp.) are glacial relicts now found only in deep rocky lakes (Figure 2). Here the hypolimnion is always well oxygenated, and during the summer the fish are thought to spend most of their time in the deep water. It seems an obvious deduction that these fish have found a cool refuge from our summer heat. Slack *et al.* (1957) observed, however, that the powan in Loch Lomond often shoal in the littoral shallows in warm water during summer, and Swift 1964, has shown that the optimum temperature for growth of Windermere char is between 12 and 16°C which he also finds to be the optimum of brown trout. Another species of *Salvelinus*, the well studied speckled trout, *S. fontinalis*, has an upper ultimate lethal temperature of 25·3°C, a temperature seldom, if ever, achieved

TABLE 4. TEMPERATURE DATA (IN °C) FOR PARTS OF THE
BRITISH ISLES (FROM TANSLEY, 1939)

	Mean of hottest month	Mean of coldest month	Mean maximum of hottest month	Mean minimum of coldest month
Extreme Atlantic climates				
Stornoway (Outer Hebrides)	12·5	4·0	15·6	1·2
Scilly Islands	16·0	7·5	18·3	5·3
West coast of England and Wales				
Southport (Lancashire)	15·2	3·7	18·5	1·4
St. Ann's Head (Pembroke)	15·0	5·7	17·1	3·8
South coast of England				
Bournemouth (Hampshire)	16·4	4·3	20·9	1·5
Dungeness (Kent)	16·4	4·0	19·5	1·5
East coast of England				
Great Yarmouth (Norfolk)	15·8	3·2	19·0	0·9
Tynemouth (Durham)	14·3	3·6	17·8	0·8
East coast of Scotland				
Leith (Midlothian)	14·7	4·0	18·7	1·0
Aberdeen	13·7	3·2	17·2	0·6
English midlands				
Oxford	16·6	3·6	21·2	0·9
Nottingham	16·1	3·0	20·9	0·3
Cambridge	16·6	3·0	22·1	0·0

in the epilimnion of our deep lakes. Thus there seems no physiological need for these fishes to retire to deep water because of temperature. Their habits and distribution illustrate a point made by Brett (1956) for North American fishes, viz. that their upper lethal temperatures determined in the laboratory are always several degrees higher than the maximum water temperatures normally encountered by the species in their areas of distribution. Since fish suffer injurious effects if kept for several weeks at high temperatures below the upper lethal temperature, one would not expect to find species forming flourishing communities where the temperature remains for several weeks near the limits of their tolerance. Usually there appears to be a large margin of safety, so that death from too high a water temperature must be extremely rare in nature. Fish are mobile and sensitive to temperature and temperature gradients; they will seek out water at preferred temperatures which are usually fairly high but well below the ultimate upper lethal level. Thus the habits of our chars and whitefishes are probably related to temperature and do result in their living in places where there is virtually no possibility of death from heat stress.

It seems unlikely that summer high temperatures by themselves act as a limit to any other of our species. Weatherley (1963) has shown that the perch is probably so limited in continental areas such as North America and Australia, where midsummer temperatures are higher than in Britain.

Lower lethal temperatures have been less extensively investigated than the upper ones and we tend to assume that all fish living in the temperate zone can survive down to 0°C and so will live under ice, provided that some water remains and that it contains dissolved oxygen. "Winter kill' is a phenomenon caused by heavy snowfalls on ice-covered ponds blocking all penetration of light. Living organisms in the water then use up oxygen in respiration and plants are not able to produce oxygen by photosynthesis, so the amount of dissolved oxygen falls and the fish die from asphyxia. This was observed in some Lake District tarns in 1941 and in many small ornamental ponds during the cold winter of 1962/1963. Apart from this, the only fish species which seems to have suffered unusual mortality in 1963 is the carp, *Cyprinus carpio*. Since this fish is extensively cultivated in ponds in eastern Europe where the climate is much more severe than in England, it seems surprising that they did not survive here.

Some of our fishes regularly undergo "overwintering" which involves reduced activity, the cessation of feeding, and the use of fat reserves to supply the energy required for the reduced rate of metabolism. Fish such as the bream do this regularly and so does the minnow, which in Windermere spends its winter under stones in shallow water, though this fish does not fast absolutely. Various Russian workers have investigated the phenomenon and have found that successful overwintering, which may well be hormonally controlled, depends on the fish having laid down adequate reserves of fat which must also be of adequate quality. If the fish are too thin at the beginning of winter, they will not survive for more than a very few days at low temperatures; for common carp, the condition factor must be at least 2·9 for the fish to overwinter (i.e. a 12-inch fish must weigh more than $1\frac{3}{4}$ lb) and the fish must not be disturbed during the cold weather or it will use its reserves too fast. Perhaps our carp died in 1963 because they were not prepared for a very cold winter because they did not feed well enough in the preceding summer. Another possible explanation is that the geographical range of this species is very great, and although it is known to "overwinter" in the northern colder parts it may not do so in the warmer southern parts. I believe many of our carp come from Italy, where they are probably active and feeding through the year; they may not have the ability to overwinter.

In physiological terms, the difference between coldwater stenotherms and eurytherms seems to lie in the adjustment of their basal metabolism to temperature. In Figure 8 the standard metabolism, which is a measure of basal metabolic rate, is shown on a semi-logarithmic grid so that its increase with higher temperature gives a shallow convex curve. The steno-thermal rainbow and speckled trouts have relatively high metabolic rates which increase only threefold between 5 and 20°C, but the eurythermal goldfish has a curve which rises steeply in the lower range of temperatures and then flattens at higher temperatures, with a total increase of about 10-fold between 5 and 20°C and 20-fold between 5 and 35°C. The chub and perch have intermediate curves. The coldwater species have a relatively high basal metabolism at low tempera-tures and so should be able to feed and remain active in cold water; often they are most active in winter. Their metabolism is already so high that they cannot survive as the temperature increases. Eurytherms such as the goldfish, on the contrary, show a considerable rise in metabolism with increase of temperature and can survive over a wide range; they are probably inactive in very cold water. The crucian carp, for instance, digs itself into the mud at the beginning of winter and falls into a state of torpor. It may even survive if the mud freezes, provided that its own body fluids remain unfrozen.

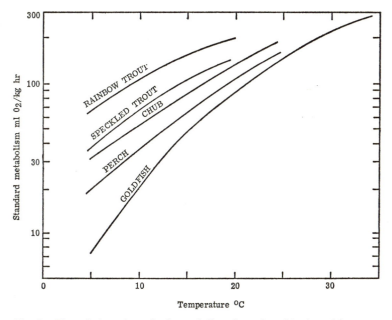

Fig. 8.—The relation of standard metabolism (on a logarithmic scale) to temperature in thermally acclimatized fish (all specimens of the order of 5 g weight). [*After Fry, 1957*]

So far, I have been discussing the effects of temperature as though this factor could be treated in isolation, but in practice changes in temperature are always accompanied by changes in the amount of oxygen dissolved in the water and this is a very important factor for many fishes. "Winter kill" is the result of asphyxia, not of cold *per se*, and death in hot water may also be the result of low oxygen concentration rather than a direct lethal effect of heat. The solubility of oxygen in water decreases with rise of temperature, so that while water at 6°C holds 12 mg/l of oxygen, that at 14°C holds only 10 mg/l, and at 26°C only 8 mg/l at normal atmospheric pressure. Basal metabolism, however, increases with rise of temperature and this mean, that the fish must consume more oxygen at higher temperaturess so that the margin of safety between oxygen requirement and oxygen availability decreases as the water becomes warmer. Where there are submerged plants in clear water in sunny weather, the water may be super-saturated with oxygen and hold more than the maximum amount expected at that temperature, but on dull days this is not possible. Where there is organic pollution or much natural decay, the amount of dissolved oxygen will be reduced below the possible maximum. Oxygen enters water by solution from the surface, especially at weirs and falls, and by secretion by plants in sunshine.

Wunder (1936) divided freshwater fishes into four categories depending on oxygen requirements; these were:—

1. Fishes normally requiring 7 to 11 cc/1 of oxygen (10 to 16 mg/1) and beginning to suffer if the concentration falls to 5 cc/1 (7 mg/1) – trout, minnow, stoneloach, bullhead.
2. Fishes requiring much oxygen but able to live with 5–7 cc/1 (7 to 10 mg/1) – grayling, chub, gudgeon, burbot, perch.
3. Fishes requiring relatively small amounts of oxygen and able to live with only 4 cc/1 (5·7 mg/1) – roach, ruffe, pike.
4. Fishes which can survive very low concentrations of oxygen, even down to $\frac{1}{2}$ cc/1 (0·7 mg/1) – carp, tench, crucian carp, bream.

These oxygen requirements are approximate values for medium temperatures for each species. The actual requirements will depend on temperature and also on the concentration of other dissolved gases which may be present, especially carbon dioxide and ammonia; the higher the concentration of these, the more oxygen is required. High concentrations of either gas may be lethal but different species have different lethal levels.

Figure 9 illustrates the relationship between temperature and oxygen requirement for rainbow trout, perch, roach and tench, fish representing Wunder's four categories. In general, at comparable temperatures, the requirements of the four species differ as Wunder predicted but there are some surprising features. Thus, for rainbow trout, the oxygen requirements for survival for $3\frac{1}{2}$ and 7 days are greater at 16°C than at 20°C – this is probably because the fish are much more active at 16 than at 20°C when left to settle down under these conditions. Perch show a similar phenomenon but it is less marked. Roach at 20°C require more oxygen to survive for 7 days than do perch at that temperature – again probably because roach are more active at this temperature than perch.

The fish with high oxygen requirements are those normally

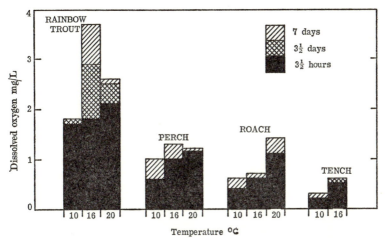

Fig. 9.—Histograms to show the relationship between oxygen requirements and temperature for four species of fish. The values shown are the minimum concentrations of dissolved oxygen at which all the individuals survived for $3\frac{1}{2}$ hours (black), $3\frac{1}{2}$ days (cross-stripes) and 7 days (stripes) at the temperatures given below the histograms. [*Drawn from data given by Downing and Merkens, 1957*]

found in fast rivers or in rocky lakes, while those with low oxygen requirements are those found in slow or stagnant waters and shallow productive lakes. There is an association, too, between oxygen requirements and temperature relations: those fish with high oxygen requirements are coldwater forms, whilst those with low requirements are eurytherms able to tolerate both high and low temperatures.

For a fish to flourish, it must be able to satisfy its full demand for oxygen at its normal full level of activity. Physiologists measure two sorts of relationship between oxygen consumption and temperature: standard metabolism and active metabolism.

The former is the oxygen consumption of an inactive fish and is virtually a measure of the basic metabolic rate, whereas the latter is the oxygen uptake of the fully active fish. The difference

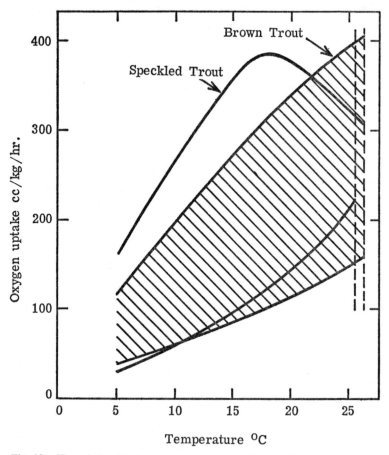

Fig. 10.—The relationship between temperature and metabolism for brown and speckled trouts. The upper lines show the active metabolism and the lower lines the standard metabolism for thermally acclimatized fish, and the areas between them (striped for brown trout, white for speckled trout) show the scope for activity. [*After Brett, 1956*]

at any temperature, between the active and standard rates of uptake is a measure of how much energy is available to the fish above its basal metabolic rate; Fry (1957) calls this the "scope for activity". Figure 10 shows curves for active and standard metabolism for brown trout and speckled trout (a char). The scope for activity of the brown trout increases with rising temperature up to the lethal level, whereas the speckled trout has a maximum scope for activity below 20°C and a relatively low scope as its lethal temperature is approached. We should expect brown trout to survive better than speckled trout where summer temperatures reach 20°C or higher, and this is probably true in North American streams.

At 10°C, trout can be fully active when the oxygen concentration is only three-quarters of saturation (7·5 mg/l) but this level of saturation at 20°C (6·7 mg/l) allows the fish to be only just over half as active as its maximum potential at that temperature. This is in clean water, but if 1 ppm of dissolved ammonia is present, the ability of the trout's blood to carry oxygen at 10°C is reduced to one seventh of the normal level. Brown trout use oxygen at the rate of 330 mg/kg/hour at 20°C and 390 mg/kg/hour at 25°C when normally active.

In a later chapter I hope to show that our fishes can be divided, on the basis of their breeding habits, into three main groups. Most of the salmonids spawn in autumn or winter when the water is cold; many cyprinids, such as bream and tench, spawn in summer when the water temperature is near its maximum; the third group, including grayling, perch, pike, bullheads and cyprinids such as minnows, barbel and chub, spawn in spring when the water is beginning to warm up. The sizes of the eggs produced by these three groups of fishes are very different, as shown in Table 5. The rate of development depends on temperature, but the figure obtained by multiplying the number of days elapsing between fertilization and hatching by the average water temperature in °C (a quantity called "degree-days") is almost constant for each species.

Brown trout take 410 degree-days within their optimum temperature range, which is 7 to 12°C; i.e., at 10°C they hatch 41 days after fertilization. Over this temperature range the alevins are the same size at hatching. Egg mortality increases above 12°C and below 7°C and those which do develop successfully produce smaller than normal alevins, presumably having consumed more energy in development so that less of the yolk is converted into fish flesh. Trout, salmon and powan eggs are killed if the temperature exceeds 14 to 16°C and this is at least partly because the passage of oxygen through the egg membrane is too slow to allow the high rate of respiration required at the high temperature. Char eggs suffer high mortality above 8°C (Swift 1965a).

Eggs of winter-breeding salmonids will survive and develop very slowly in water down to 0°C. Assuming average water

TABLE 5. THE EGG SIZE (AS MM DIAMETER) AND TIME NEEDED
FOR DEVELOPMENT (AS DEGREE-DAYS BETWEEN FERTILIZATION AND
HATCHING) FOR VARIOUS BRITISH FRESHWATER FISHES

	Egg size (mm)	Degree-days (°C)
Autumn and winter spawners		
Salmon	5–7	420
Brown trout	4–5·5	410
Char	4	390–460
Powan	3	425–500
Spring spawners		
Grayling	3–4	200
Pike	2·5–3	80–160
Perch	2–2·5	120–260
Bullhead	2–2·5	
Barbel	2	
Minnow	1·3–1·4	
Summer spawners		
Stickleback	1·5–1·7	
Bream	1·5	
Tench	1·2	
Carp	0·9–1·2	60–90
Ruffe	0·5–1	

temperatures of 6°C, the time taken to hatch will be of the order of 10 weeks; it may be much longer if the water is colder, but it is unlikely to be less than 6 or 7 weeks even in chalk streams. Thus the eggs will normally hatch in early spring.

Most of the spring spawners probably do not spawn until the water temperature is at least 10°C. Their eggs are mostly between 2 and 3 mm in diameter and therefore contain less yolk than those of the winter spawners. Swift (1956) quotes figures showing very high mortality for pike eggs below 6° and above 16°C and for perch eggs below 8° and above 20°C; mortality was high (more than 38%) in all his batches of eggs. With an average water temperature of about 12°C, eggs of spring spawners will hatch in 10 to 18 days, i.e. in late spring or early summer.

The summer spawners have even smaller eggs, less than 2 mm in diameter. Their development has been studied very little except for that of the carp. This fish usually spawns only if the water temperature exceeds 18°C; at 20°C, the eggs would hatch after 3 days. The eggs and young of carp must have high upper lethal temperature limits, since this fish can spawn in tropical fish ponds at temperatures round 30°C. It is probable that the lower lethal temperature limits for eggs and fry are much higher than those of the adult fish.

Very little is known of the physiology of alevins (the yolked young which hatch from the eggs) and young fry (the early feeding stage), but Bishai (1960a,b) has investigated the temperature and dissolved oxygen relations of young salmon and trout. Newly hatched alevins of both species, from eggs incubated at 6°C, had upper lethal temperatures of 23°C, measured as median survival over a seven-day period. This can be compared with lethal temperatures of 16°C for the eggs; alevins have no egg membrane to slow down the passage of oxygen. Older alevins were slightly less tolerant and showed a small effect of acclimatization if kept at 20°C compared with 5°C.

Newly hatched salmon alevins can survive for 20 hours at 5°C with only 2·8 per cent saturation of oxygen (0·3 mg/l) and brown trout are almost as hardy, but sea-trout alevins require more dissolved oxygen. The amount required increases with age, becoming about 16 per cent saturation at 6°C (1·9 mg/l) when they are ready to feed and 24 per cent (2·9 mg/l) for feeding fry; these concentrations allow survival for at least 48 hours. Alevins and young fry were not injured when exposed to high concentrations of dissolved oxygen – more than 350 per cent saturation at 6° and 15°C for 3 and 5 days respectively (equivalent to more than 40 mg/l).

Thus from their oxygen requirements and their relation to temperature, we can grade our fishes between two extreme types, the coldwater stenotherms with high oxygen consumption and the eurytherms with very low oxygen consumption. The former must be confined to waters where there is nearly always at least 5 cc/l (7 mg/l) of dissolved oxygen and the temperature seldom rises above 20°C, and this is consistent with their presence in deep rocky lakes and in the swift upper reaches of rivers. The eurytherms could live in these waters, too, but those with very low oxygen requirements are usually found only in slow-moving or still waters where the oxygen falls to low values and the temperature may rise above 25°C.

Between these extremes we find a series of fishes, each with a characteristic oxygen requirement and temperature tolerance and each found in a characteristic water type. Few, if any, of these are limited by temperature conditions but those with higher oxygen requirements may be unable to live in certain environments, e.g. chub, perch and grayling could not live in some of the waters occupied by tench and bream. We can thus explain why some fishes with narrow limits of tolerance, i.e. high oxygen requirements, do not live in some waters; but the eurythermal fishes with low oxygen requirements could, in theory, live in any of our waters. Why are their distributions limited? We must seek the explanation in other facets of their lives and especially in their breeding and feeding habits.

Human activities involve much use of water. Considerable quantities are abstracted, leading to lessened flow in rivers; some is returned to the rivers after use but never entirely unchanged. At the very best, it is heated or else enriched with mineral salts as the result of passing through a sewage disposal works; often it carries a load of organic pollution which causes a drop in the oxygen concentration of the river into which it is discharged. These changes, in the direction of higher temperature and less dissolved oxygen, will make the waters concerned less suitable for the coldwater fishes such as salmonids, even though they are usually still tolerable for many cyprinid fishes. Thus the spread of industries and of domestic plumbing is narrowing the range of some of our fishes but allowing an increase in range to others. In angling terms, the game fisherman finds his waters restricted, unless special precautions are taken, but the coarse fisherman may find that carp, bream and tench fishing is improving and spreading.

Chapter 3

The distribution of freshwater fishes in relation to topography

A NY experienced angler can stand beside a piece of water in Britain and then tell you what species of fish he would expect to find there – and he is usually right. If he is wrong, it is probably because geological and climatic changes during the past million years have led to species being unable to reach the water, although they could flourish there. Man has often introduced species which he thought would survive and be useful as food or for sport, so there is a certain arbitrariness about the distribution of our freshwater fishes. This is well illustrated in Ireland where probably only salmonid fishes are truly native, having arrived there by their natural methods of dispersal, and all others have been introduced.

Very few species of fish can live in every possible freshwater habitat; perhaps the eel is the most versatile of our fishes. The brown trout has quite a wide range of possible habitats, for it can live in small streams, large slow rivers, small tarns, large lakes and even in estuaries; the minnow, also, has a wide range; other fishes have quite restricted habitats, for instance the barbel in our southern rivers.

One of the first attempts to classify flowing waters according to the fish which are likely to live in them was made by Kathleen Carpenter in 1928. She divided a typical river into:

1. The *"headstream"* or *"highland brook"*, which is small, often torrential and usually very cold. Trout and salmon parr may live here but no other fishes.
2. The *"troutbeck"*, which is slightly larger than the headstream but still torrential and rocky. Only the trout and salmon parr live in the open water but the bullhead may shelter among the stones.
3. The *"minnow reach"*, which is still fairly swift but in which there are patches of mud and silt in places protected from the current and a few rooted plants,

TABLE 6. HUET'S CLASSIFICATION OF EUROPEAN RIVER ZONES (HUET, 1949, 1954)

	Trout zone	*Grayling** (Minnow) zone	*Barbel** (Chub) zone	*Bream zone*
Gradient	very steep	steep	gentle	very gentle
Current	very rapid	rapid	moderate	slow
Type of fish fauna	salmonid	mixed, with salmonids predominating	mixed, with cyprinids predominating	cyprinid, with predators

Fishes usually present (those underlined are most common; those in square brackets are uncommon)

	Trout zone	*Grayling** (Minnow) zone	*Barbel** (Chub) zone	*Bream zone*
	<u>trout</u>, <u>salmon parr</u>, minnow, bullhead, stoneloach	fish of trout zone <u>grayling*</u> cyprinids of running water [complementary cyprinids] [complementary predators]	[fish of trout zone] [grayling] cyprinids of running water complementary cyprinids complementary predators [cyprinids of still water]	[cyprinids of running water] complementary cyprinids complementary predators cyprinids of still water

Cyprinids of running water include: barbel*, chub, dace, gudgeon, bleak.
Complementary cyprinids include: rudd, roach.
Complementary predators include: perch, pike, eel.
Cyprinids of still water include: tench, bream, white bream, carp.
* The grayling and barbel have limited distributions in British waters but are much more common in continental rivers.

such as the water buttercup, are able to grow. Trout, salmon and minnows are common here and also the bullhead.

4. The *"lowland reach"*, which is slow and meandering with a muddy bottom and many rooted plants. Here we typically find "coarse" fishes, e.g. mainly cyprinids.

Huet (1949, 1954) has set up a similar system for European continental waters and supports his classification by quoting definite values for gradient, width of river and so on. He divides his rivers into four main zones, summarized in Table 6:

1. The *"trout zone"*, with salmonids dominating the fauna (equivalent to the troutbeck).
2. The *"grayling zone"*, with a fauna of salmonids, cyprinids and others, but the trout or grayling is the most abundant (dominant) fish. The cyprinids of this zone are mainly the barbel, chub and dace, but roach and rudd may be present and possibly also the predatory fishes, pike, perch and eel. This zone is roughly the same as the minnow reach.
3. The *"barbel zone"*, with a mixed fauna dominated by cyprinids. Trout and grayling may still be present but barbel and chub are the characteristic fishes, with roach and rudd fairly abundant and occasional carp, tench and bream. The predatory fishes – pike, perch and eel – are fairly abundant.
4. The *"bream zone"*, having characteristically a fauna of cyprinids with predatory fishes also present. The characteristic cyprinids are the roach, rudd, carp, tench and bream.

Huet finds that rivers of like breadth, depth and gradient have identical biological properties and specially similar fish populations (provided that they are in the same bio-geographical area). Figure 11 shows his correlation between gradient, width and fish fauna. He comments that a stream 15 yards wide will be part of the trout zone if the gradient is 8‰ or more, part of the grayling (minnow) zone if the gradient is 4‰, part of the barbel (chub) zone if the gradient is 1½‰, and part of the bream zone if the gradient is only 0·25‰. If

the gradient is 2‰ the river will be barbel (chub) zone if it is
10 yards wide but grayling (minnow) zone if it is 40 yards wide.

The gradient of a river is correlated with the shape of the
river valley. Rivers in V-shaped valleys with steep slopes are
characteristically trout waters; where the valley is wider, with
gentler slopes, we find rivers of the grayling (minnow) zone;
in wide shallow valleys, the meandering rivers usually harbour

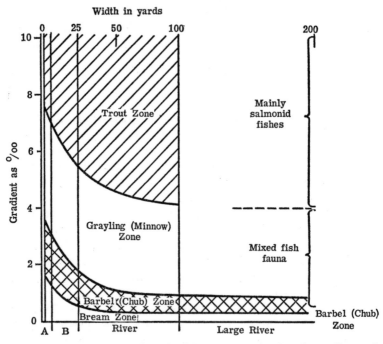

Fig. 11.—Diagram to show how the fish zones are related to the gradient and
width of flowing waters: A—brook (up to 5 yards wide); B—little river (between
5 and 25 yards wide). [*After Huet, 1949*]

the fishes of the barbel (chub) zone, whereas the bream zone
is found where the land is flat and the river meanders slowly,
leaving ox-bows and old stagnant courses. Huet comments
that grayling and barbel are seldom found in streams less than
5 yards wide even if the other conditions seem suitable. Perhaps
it is because of this that they are comparatively rare in our
rivers, so that we should re-name the grayling and barbel zones
the minnow and chub zones respectively.

The fish zone depends very largely on gradient and all zones may not be represented in one river or in the same order in all rivers. Thus many Scottish and Irish rivers consist entirely of trout zone throughout their lengths. In other rivers, rapid shallow reaches of greater gradient may alternate with slow deep reaches of slight gradient, so that grayling (minnow) zones may alternate and lie downstream of barbel (chub) zones or even bream zones. The Derbyshire River Derwent shows clearly this alternation of deep and shallow reaches.

How does the topography of rivers affect the fishes living in them? Huet (1962) has discussed at length the effects of current on organisms living in fresh water. Water flow is certainly an important factor and related to it are the type of sediment, the flora and the invertebrate fauna. The temperature and oxygen regimes of a river may also depend on its current. Since greater gradients and therefore faster currents are found in mountainous regions, which in the British Isles are mostly composed of non-calcareous rocks, there are chemical differences between our fast and slow rivers. The latter are usually in regions of calcareous rocks surrounded by rich, agricultural land.

Fish which live in swiftly flowing water must be able to maintain their positions against the current and to move upstream to counteract the effects of being swept downstream. They must expend muscular energy to do this. Their bodies are usually stream-lined and round or oval in cross-section (Figure 12) in contrast to the deep-bodied, laterally flattened fishes of slow-moving or still waters. Table 7 (from Kreitmann, 1932)

TABLE 7. MAXIMUM SUSTAINED SWIMMING SPEEDS OF FRESHWATER FISHES (KREITMANN, 1932)

Species	Speed (m/sec)	Species	Speed (m/sec)
Salmon	8·00	Bleak	0·60
Brown trout	4·40	Bream	0·60
Chub	2·70	Tench	0·47
Barbel	2·40	Pike	0·45
Dace	1·80	Carp	0·40

shows how the swimming speeds of freshwater fishes vary. Fishermen will have noticed the differences between the staying power of some of these fishes; thus, the carp and bream

make vigorous efforts to escape capture but cannot sustain
them for long, barbel and chub put up a long fight but then
tire, whereas the bleak (like the trout) continues to fight to the
end. The deep-bodied fishes simply could not survive in swift
rivers, for they cannot maintain the effort needed to breast the

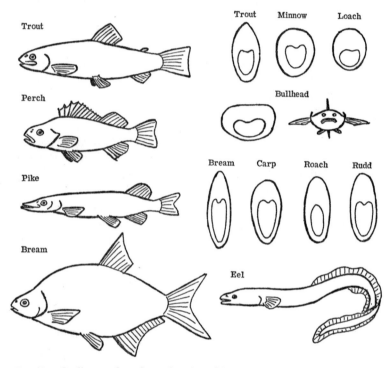

Fig. 12.—Outlines and sections of various fishes to illustrate different habits of
life. The trout, minnow and loach live in rapid water and swim well; the bullhead
lives on the bottom in rapid water; the perch is a moderate swimmer; the pike
is a lurking predator which can make rapid darts, like an arrow; the bream,
carp, roach and rudd live in slowly flowing or still waters; the eel is almost
ubiquitous.

current. Some of the fish of swift rivers avoid the current by
living on the bottom and these are often dorso-ventrally
flattened, as is the bullhead. The eel can also live on the bottom
and wind its way among boulders, pushing itself upstream
rather like a snake. On the other hand, deep-bodied fishes can
move more easily through weeds than those with round cross-

sections, but the eel does this very well, too. The pike is an arrow-shaped predator capable of rapid darts but not of sustained high speed or of rapid twists and turns. It is ideally shaped for lurking among not too dense weeds.

Invertebrates living in swift water also show adaptations to the eroded substratum and ever-present current. Stoneflies, flat-bodied mayflies, limpets and *Simulium* (reed smut) larvae are characteristic animals. Where the current is less swift, sand, silt and mud accumulate and in these depositing substrata live completely different animals such as chironomid larvae and burrowing, silt-loving mayflies and large mussels. Plants need some silt for their roots, so they are much more common and much more luxuriant in the slower reaches of the rivers. The

TROUT ZONE   BREAM ZONE

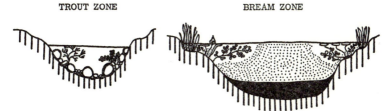

Fig. 13. Sections (not to scale) through the trout and bream zones of rivers to show difference in substratum (black is mud), in vegetation, and in dissolved oxygen conditions in summer (white indicates plenty of dissolved oxygen, dots indicate little or none).

stones of small swift streams are covered with green algae in summer and the moss *Fontinalis antipyreticum* may form a dense carpet sheltering chironomid larvae and pea mussels. The large flowering plants of sluggish rivers may support many animals and also provide shelter for small crustaceans such as clado-cerans and copepods. Detritus from decaying plants and fallen leaves may support a rich fauna of crustaceans such as the shrimp and slater, various caddises and mayflies. Hynes (1963) believes that this detritus is the basis of the food chains in most flowing fresh waters. In large deep rivers, the plants are con-fined to the shallow water near the banks but there may be a rich fauna in the bottom mud of the middle.

Huet's fish zones thus represent also a series of plant zones and invertebrate animal zones, summarized in Table 8 and Figure 13. The salmonid fishes are generally associated with a

poor flora and a fauna largely adapted to clinging to and
crawling over stones; the fact that the fish commonly supple-
ment this diet with insects which fall into the water is exploited
by the fly fisherman. The cyprinid fishes, however, usually live
where plants are abundant and the invertebrates live on or in
them or burrowing in the silted bottom.

TABLE 8. GENERAL CHARACTERISTICS OF THE FISH ZONES OF FLOWING
WATERS

	ZONE			
	Trout	*Minnow*	*Chub*	*Bream*
Gradient	very steep	steep	gentle	very gentle
Current	very rapid	rapid	moderate	slow
Eroded bottom (stones, gravel)	+++	++	+	—
Depositing bottom (sand, mud)	—	+	++	+++
Summer temperatures	cool	fairly cool	warm	hot
Dissolved oxygen in summer	plenty	plenty	some	little
Water plants present:				
submerged	+	++	++	++ or —
emergent	—	+	++	++
floating	—	—	++	++ or —
Invertebrate animals:				
clinging and crawling	+++	++	+	—
plant-living	+	++	+++	++ or —
burrowing or buried	—	+	++	+++

To complete the survey of fresh waters, we must include
still waters. These vary in area, in depth and in profile. One
extreme type, such as Ennerdale Water or Wastwater in the
Lake District, is deep and has steep sides so that there is very
little shallow water (the littoral zone) compared with the area
of deep water. By contrast with this, south-country reservoirs
such as Blagdon, Chew Valley, Weir Wood, and the Norfolk
Broads (which are flooded medieval peat diggings) are shallow
and consist very largely of littoral zone. Intermediate conditions
are illustrated by lakes such as Windermere and Loch Lomond,
which have slightly more shallow water than Wastwater,
while Lough Derg and Malham Tarn, for instance, have more

shallow than deep water. The deep lakes lie in mountainous country, whereas shallow lakes are usually surrounded by gently rolling agricultural land. The fish faunas are quite different. Deep lakes are typically salmonid waters with trout, char and whitefishes as the dominant fish, whereas shallow lakes are cyprinid waters with bream, tench and carp as the characteristic fish. Intermediate types of lake contain mixed populations, with perch and pike often present in great numbers.

Thus the lakes of V-shaped valleys are salmonid waters, as are the streams flowing through such valleys. Where the valley slopes are more gentle, predatory perch and pike join the salmonids, and with still more gentle slopes, roach and rudd join the perch and pike and the salmonids may disappear. Where the land is rolling rather than hilly, the lakes, like the rivers, are dominated by cyprinids such as bream and tench.

The different lake types are associated with different floras and faunas, summarized in Table 9 and Figure 14. The salmonid

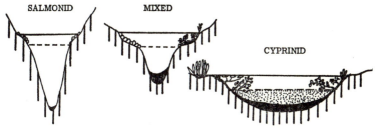

Fig. 14.—Sections (not to scale) through typical lakes with salmonid, mixed or cyprinid faunas, to show differences in substratum (black is mud), in vegetation, and in dissolved oxygen conditions in summer (white indicates plenty of oxygen and dots indicate little or none). The horizontal broken lines represent the position of the thermocline in summer.

lakes with rocky or stony shores and few rooted plants in the limited littoral zone form a great contrast to the shallow cyprinid lakes with muddy bottoms and abundant growth of higher plants; these are usually present as a ring of emergent plants such as reeds and rushes, surrounding water with both submerged and floating vegetation. The plankton, consisting of small floating plants and animals, provides in lakes a food supply which in rivers is found only in sheltered weed beds and backwaters. Phyto- and zooplankton are abundant in deep rocky lakes in spring and summer. Animals such as limpets, stoneflies and mayflies crawl over the bottom of the narrow littoral zone, and the muddy bottom of the deep water supports varied chironomids. There may be a very rich summer growth of phytoplankton in the shallow lakes, and small crustaceans and rotifers live among the rooted plants as well as in the

TABLE 9. GENERAL CHARACTERISTICS OF THE THREE LAKE TYPES

Type of fish fauna	*Salmonid*	*Mixed*	*Cyprinid*
Proportion of deep water	+++	++	—
Proportion of shallow water	—	+ or ++	+++
Amount of dissolved oxygen in the hypolimnion in summer	plenty	plenty	none
Littoral zone:			
of stones and gravel	++	+	—
of sand and mud	—	+	+
Rooted plants	—	+	+++
Phytoplankton	+	++	+++
Invertebrate animals:			
crawling in shallow water	++	++	—
burrowing in sand or mud	—	++	+++
living on and among plants	—	+	+++
in zooplankton	+	++	++
Characteristic fishes:	trout char whitefishes minnow bullhead	perch pike sticklebacks with some salmonids or some cyprinids	roach rudd tench carp

zooplankton. Snails, caddises and other insect larvae crawl over the plants and chironomids burrow in the mud.

There are differences in temperature and in oxygen content which can be associated with topographical differences between waters. Small streams are generally at greater altitudes than large rivers, and the average temperature increases downstream as the river gets larger. A slow-flowing river has more time to warm up, and if it has a greater volume will cool down less overnight than smaller faster rivers. The bream zone is also more likely to receive effluents from sewage disposal works or factories and these usually contribute warmth, so there may be a difference in temperature of several degrees between the different fish zones of one river. Salmonids are less tolerant of high temperatures than cyprinids, so their distribution through the fish zones is consistent with the summer temperatures prevailing in them (see Chapter 2).

For various reasons the amount of dissolved oxygen is likely to be less in slow, deep rivers than in shallow, fast ones. There are two sources of oxygenation: first, through the water surface, especially where there is turbulence, and secondly, from submerged plants which produce oxygen as the result of photosynthesis.

The trout zone with its rapid and often turbulent flow is usually well oxygenated. In the minnow zone the turbulence is less than upstream but there may be many submerged plants, so the oxygen content is likely to remain high. Emergent and floating leaves of plants do not contribute oxygen to the water. Effluents, even those of high quality, usually use up some oxygen from the water, so lower reaches receiving these tend to be depleted more than upper cleaner ones. In any case, since the water receiving these effluents is warmer, it can hold less oxygen. In deep wide rivers with plants only at the verge and muddy bottoms with many burrowing animals, the water is likely to become markedly depleted of oxygen and has little opportunity of acquiring more except at weirs, which are infrequent because of the small gradient. The fishes of the bream zone, living in these conditions, are all capable of existing with very little dissolved oxygen (see Figure 13).

The temperature regime of lakes follows an annual cycle. In spring, the sun warms the surface waters and if the weather is calm an upper layer of warm water develops and floats on the colder, denser water below it (see Figure 7). There is a sudden change of temperature at the level (the thermocline) separating these two layers. The warm upper layer (epilimnion) and cold lower layer (hypolimnion) usually remain separate through the summer, but in the autumn the upper layer cools and winds cause an "overturn" so that the two layers become mixed and the whole lake assumes almost the same temperature. If the winter is cold so that the temperature falls below 4°C, an upper layer of cold water may begin to float on the heavier water at 4°C below it and ice may eventually cover the surface, while if the lake is sufficiently deep the water at the bottom may still be at 4°C. In temperate latitudes, all lakes stratify in summer unless they are very shallow (less than 6 to 10 feet deep), but these shallow lakes will warm up to the bottom. Small lakes will tend to warm up faster than large ones and to cool faster in winter.

The temperature regime affects the oxygen regime. When the lake is mixed, with no thermocline and temperatures either uniform or falling steadily from top to bottom, there is a free circulation of substances in solution through all the layers and all the water is probably well oxygenated. Once the thermocline develops, the exchange of dissolved substances between the epilimnion and hypolimnion stops almost completely. Photosynthesis is active in the phytoplankton of the epilimnion and this layer remains well oxygenated. The fate of the hypolimnion depends on its volume and on the productivity of the water. If the water is very productive, dead material accumulates at the bottom and its decay uses up oxygen; also, many burrowing organisms may live in the bottom and use up oxygen, and so the amount of oxygen in the hypolimnion will be greatly reduced and may fall to zero. In less productive water less oxygen is used up, and where the lake is very deep the volume of the hypolimnion may be very large compared with the area of bottom, so the water will not become deoxygenated and may retain quite large concentrations of oxygen through the summer. During the autumn overturn, when the two layers mix, the hypolimnion becomes well oxygenated once more and the nutrients which have accumulated in it are shared with the epilimnion. The mixing is therefore often followed by an outburst of phyto- and zooplankton if the weather becomes fine in October.

Conditions in the epilimnion will remain suitable for fishes throughout the year, as far as oxygen is concerned, but the water may become too hot for some. The hypolimnion remains cool through the summer but it may become depleted of oxygen and thus tolerable only for fishes with very low requirements. In deep, rocky, unproductive lakes, fishes such as char, trout, perch and pike can live in the hypolimnion through the summer; in shallower, productive lakes, these fish will be

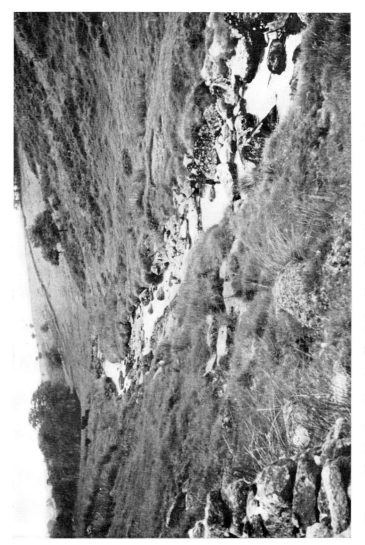

Plate 1.—*The West Dart River above Two Bridges (Devonshire).* This is the upper end of the *trout zone* where the gradient is steep, the current is swift and the substratum consists of boulders, stones and gravel.

Plate 2.—*The Afon Elan in central Wales (Radnorshire)*. This is typical of the *trout zone*. There are many gravelly areas which are ideal spawning sites for trout.

Plate 3.—*The River Wye above Rhayader (Radnorshire).* This is a famous trout stream, flowing through a steep-sided valley and typical of the *lower trout zone.*

Plate 4.—*The River Coln at Bibury (Gloucestershire)*. This is another famous trout stream but differs greatly from the R. Wye because it is spring-fed. There is always a good flow of water and the temperature varies relatively little through the year; the bottom consists of stones and gravel but there are many clumps of submerged plants. The surrounding limestone hills are much more fertile than the granite mountains of Wales.

Plate 5.—*The River Yarty near Axminster (Devonshire)*. If this river were wider it would be very typical of the *grayling zone*; the gradient is moderately steep and the bottom consists of gravel and stones with many submerged plants. The locality is further west than the natural distribution of the grayling in Britain. Salmon, sea trout and brown trout flourish in this small river.

Plate 6.—*The River Thames at Godstow (Berkshire and Oxfordshire).* This is the *barbel (chub) zone* and both these species can be observed spawning in shallow water about half a mile downstream. The wide river meanders across a wide valley, but the current is moderate and shallow stony reaches alternate with deep muddy pools where good bream are to be found.

Plate 7.—*The Great Ouse River at St. Neots* (*Huntingdonshire*). This is typical of the *bream zone*, with the deep river flowing slowly through rich pastures. The bottom consists largely of soft mud, and plants are restricted to the edges.

72

Plate 8.—*The River Trent at Swarkeston (Derbyshire)*. This is the *barbel (chub) zone*; the river is wide with a moderate current and it flows through good agricultural land. Unfortunately, this river has suffered more than most from industrial pollution; the picture shows the detergent foam as the water swirls over boulders in the shallower part.

73

Plate 9.—*Loch Rannoch* (*Perthshire*). This is a narrow deep lake with stony wave-washed shores—a typical unproductive lake. Brown trout are the principal fish here but pike are also present. The surrounding countryside consists largely of moor and forest.

Plate 10.—*Loch Tummel* (*Perthshire*). This lake is further down the valley than Loch Rannoch and its surroundings are less bleak. Brown trout are numerous; perch are present as well as pike.

Plate 11.—*Blenheim Lake, Woodstock (Oxfordshire).* This artificial lake is shallow with a muddy bottom. Plants grow profusely and tench and bream flourish in this highly productive lake.

76

Plate 12.—*Lochan an Daim* (*Perthshire*). This small pond has brown peaty water which is very soft and contains organic acids. There is a small inflowing stream with much gravel so trout spawn freely and the lochan is full of small brown trout.

Plate 13.—*The brown trout Salmo trutta.* The large eye and mouth at the most forward end of the body are characteristic of carnivorous fish hunting by sight. The streamlined body, large tail, large and flexible first dorsal and paired fins give the fish great manoeuvrability. The small second dorsal (adipose) fin can be seen against the boulder—in the British Isles adipose fins are found only on salmonid fishes.

Plate 14.—*Two views of a female brown trout "cutting a redd" in a shallow aquarium.*
Trout spawn on stony, gravelly bottoms where a water current passes through the
stones. The female makes a shallow pit by moving stones by energetic lateral
movements of the tail. The male remains in attendance but drives away other
males.

Plate 15.—"*Eyed ova*" *of the brown trout.* These eggs are about ½ cm (⅕ inch) in diameter. The embryo develops using the supply of yolk and these are almost ready to hatch. The small fish have large, well-developed eyes. The yolk includes oil globules.

Plate 16.—"*Alevin*" *of the brown trout.* After hatching, the young trout continues to live on its yolk and moves away from the light into the gravel bottom. When the yolk is nearly used up, it moves up towards the light and begins to feed on drifting particles. The alevin in the picture is nearly ready to feed and just over 2 cm (⅘ inch) long. The yolk is carried from the yolk sac to the body by two large blood vessels, one of which is clearly visible.

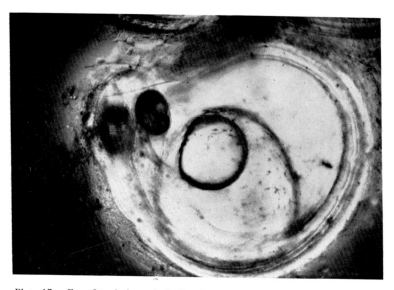

Plate 17.—*Egg of perch, Perca fluviatilis, about to hatch.* The outside of the egg is sticky, so some debris has become attached to it. The most conspicuous parts of the perch embryo are the large eyes and the oil globule in the yolk sac.

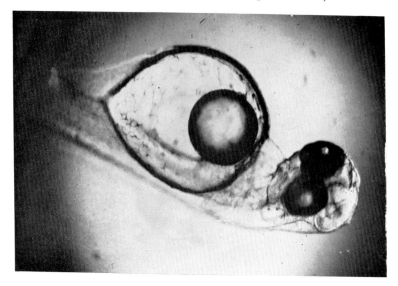

Plate 18.—*"Alevin" of perch, immediately after hatching.* The yolk sac, containing the large oil globule, provides food for the young fish. The eyes and the brain are relatively enormous; the heart can be seen between the eyes and yolk sac, and contracts, actively forcing the blood from the vitelline veins round the body.

Plate 19.—*An example of a food chain.* The picture shows the remains of a rainbow trout (*Salmo gairdneri*) which has been left by an otter on the embankment of a reservoir. The trout had been feeding on the fry of roach (*Rutilus rutilus*) and had eaten a surprising number of these small fish.

Plate 20.—*Another food chain.* This 4 lb 6 oz, pike from Windermere had swallowed whole a trout weighing 10 oz.

Photo by courtesy of Dr W. E. Frost.

Plate 21.—*A group of fish (pike, trout and perch) in an aquarium.* These species live together in lakes such as Loch Tummel and Windermere. The pike show the characteristic waiting attitude; the others are small fishes lurking close to the bottom.

Photo by courtesy of Mr K. E. Marshall.

84

Plate 22.—*Trout, "char" and perch in an aquarium.* One perch has its large spiny dorsal fin expanded; the picture shows that this fish has large eyes and differs from trout and pike in having its pelvic fins almost below the pectoral fins. The char (actually an American speckled "trout") is patterned with light spots against a dark background in contrast to the brown trout which has dark spots against a pale background. *Photo by courtesy of Mr. K. E. Marshall.*

confined to the epilimnion but cyprinids such as the carp and tench, with very low oxygen requirements, will continue to be able to feed on the muddy bottom of the almost deoxygenated hypolimnion (see Figure 14). Deep unproductive lakes therefore offer a refuge from the heat of summer to fishes with high oxygen requirements, whereas the fishes of shallow productive lakes must be able to tolerate either high summer temperatures or low oxygen concentrations – or both.

Thus the distinction between the faunas of salmonid and cyprinid lakes can be related to the physiology of those fishes, in so far as the salmonids may not be able to tolerate the conditions in cyprinid lakes. Reasons for the absence of cyprinids from salmonid lakes must be sought in their breeding and feeding habits, particularly in relation to the flora and invertebrate fauna, which are important to fishes in many ways. The most obvious one is as food, which I shall discuss later. Plants may provide shelter, and this may be very important to adult fishes in their daily lives, for example to the lurking predatory pike. Many of our fishes spawn among weeds and attach their sticky eggs to rooted plants, and the young fry of many species find food and shelter in weed beds. All these fish, and they include most of our cyprinids, could not complete their life cycles in flowing waters or in still waters without sufficient rooted plants, e.g. in the trout zone of rivers or in deep, rocky lakes. The salmonid fishes and others such as the minnow lay their eggs among stones and gravel and can spawn only where suitable gravel patches are available; they therefore cannot spawn in weedy waters with bottoms of deep mud or earth. Salmonid fishes, however, may move far from their breeding grounds and are often migratory in habit. They can feed in the chub and bream zones of rivers or in silted weedy lakes and can maintain a population in such waters, provided that they have access to suitable spawning streams to which they move in autumn.

Some cyprinids have the body form of active swimmers, e.g. chub, dace, barbel, and these could undertake migrations similar to those of the trout, but I know of no information about this in our waters. Fishes related to the barbel undertake spawning migrations in other parts of the world. The deep-bodied cyprinids, however, have not the shape to swim great distances although they congregate in suitable places to breed and may move up and down rivers to some extent. Where effluents entering rivers cause varying degrees of pollution fishes such as roach are sometimes present and sometimes absent.

Chapter 4

The annual climatic cycle and its effect on freshwater fishes

The British climate is a "temperate" one, without extremes, because of our position beside the Atlantic Ocean and in the path of the West Wind Drift (Gulf Stream). The number of hours of daylight (which I shall call daylength) varies regularly, with a minimum just before Christmas and a maximum just before Midsummer Day, and the elevation of the sun at mid-day is least during the shortest day and greatest at the longest. This annual cycle is of great importance to plants since the intensity of sunlight determines the amount of photosynthesis. Many of them lose their leaves or die back in autumn to grow vigorously again the following spring. Since all animals depend ultimately on plants as their source of energy, the annual variation in plant growth may have direct effects on fishes through their food supply. Some fishes eat plants, many of them eat herbivorous animals, and others eat decaying plant material or animals feeding on this detritus, but none of our fishes are entirely herbivorous.

The air temperature varies fairly regularly through the year and is usually highest in July and August and lowest in February. Water temperatures are generally related to air temperatures (as already discussed) so there is an annual variation in water temperature, with the maximum coming after the longest daylength and the minimum after the shortest daylength.

Our rainfall is another variable phenomenon, but on the whole it is heaviest in autumn and winter. We are likely to have some rain in every month of the year but we do sometimes suffer from droughts of several weeks' duration. Rainfall affects freshwater animals by altering the level of water, its volume and its flow. Effects are greatest in "flashy" streams and rivers on impervious rocks, and here the movement of the rocky bottom deposits may result in a sparse fauna and poor growth of the characteristic fishes – usually trout.

All our fishes and many of our freshwater animals show an annual periodicity in breeding and growth, as illustrated by

TABLE 10. GENERAL SUMMARY OF ANNUAL CYCLES IN BRITISH FRESHWATERS

	Jan. Feb. Mar. Apr. May June July Aug. Sept. Oct. Nov. Dec.
Daylength	Increasing ————————→ long, decreasing ————————→ short
Temperature	cold, rising ————————————→ hot, falling ————————→
Food organisms—	
aquatic:	
plants	begin to grow ——→ luxuriant —— die back
chironomids	a series of generations through the year
other insects	nymphs grow → adults: eggs ————————→ hatch, nymphs grow
shrimps, slaters	adults breed and grow fast ———————— grow slowly
snails	adults ———— breed, die: eggs → hatch, young grow fast
zooplankton	scarce ————→ abundant locally ———————— scarce
terrestrial:	
mainly insects	none some maximum none
Fish growth cycles	
salmonids	slow ————→ rapid growth —— (check) — growth slows/stops
perch	none rapid growth ———————— growth stops
roach	none rapid growth ———————— growth slows
bream	none rapid growth —— growth stops

Table 10 and Figure 15. Indeed, for determining the age of fishes we rely on the annual alternation of wide and narrow, or dense and clear, structure in skeletal tissues such as opercular bones, fin-rays, vertebral centra and, above all, scales. For some fishes, this regular alternation of structure corresponds with a regular alternation between rapid and slow growth, as with trout and perch, but for others the annual "check" coincides with the spawning season and the beginning of rapid growth following this, as in most cyprinids.

Brown trout show an annual cycle of growth, typically with the most rapid increase in early summer, a check in autumn and very little or no growth in winter. (Mature trout spawn in November and December.) There may be local variations, with a check in July followed by increased growth, or increased growth for a short period in late September following a late

summer check. Swift (1961) thinks these can all be explained
by the annual temperature cycle in fresh water, and I agree
that temperature variations have an important effect on trout
growth, but I suspect that light is also involved since growth

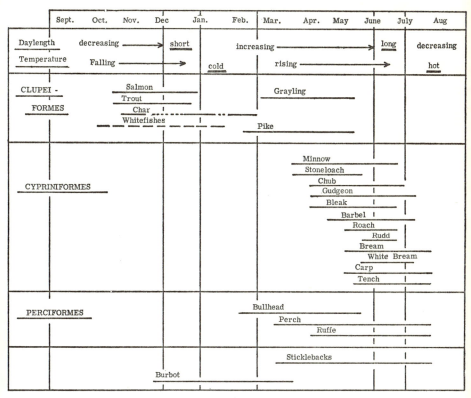

Fig. 15.—Diagram to show the breeding seasons of British freshwater fishes, with
special reference to annual cycles of daylight and water temperature. The
horizontal lines indicate the dates when breeding individuals are likely to be
found. [*Based on many sources, of varying reliability*]

often starts in spring at a time when water temperatures are
still low but daylength and light intensity have increased.
Campbell (1963) has recorded good growth in brown trout
in Loch Garry, Inverness-shire, after impoundment, in March,
when the water temperature was less than 4°C. Perch do not
grow in the autumn and winter and growth starts in April (in
Windermere).

Fish cannot grow unless they eat more food than is needed to satisfy their maintenance requirements (i.e. to provide energy for their normal activity and for their basal metabolism), so it is obvious that a fasting fish cannot increase in weight except by imbibing water. So those fish that fast or feed little during the winter, such as bream, silver bream, roach, bleak and rudd, can grow little if at all in winter; all their growth must take place during spring and summer. It is only fish which are feeding well that are likely to grow fast, but trout that are given plenty of food do not use it as efficiently as those allowed restricted rations (but more than the maintenance require-ment), so it is difficult to describe growth entirely in terms of the amount of food eaten. The initial spurt in growth at the begin-ning of the season may be the result of using food very efficiently at that time, but many forms of food are present in greater amount and variety in early spring than at any other time of year.

Steady growth through the summer can only be related to an abundant food supply if the diet consists of plankton, plants, crustaceans, or insects such as chironomids, of which there is a succession of species emerging as adults at intervals during the summer and so providing an abundant and continuous source of food in the form of large larvae. Food of terrestrial origin, too, is likely to be most abundant in summer as adult insects such as beetles and aphids. Investigators of almost all fishes have found their stomachs fuller and more of them full in May and June than at any other times of the year.

The annual growth cycles are likely to be more closely related to temperature than to any other factor, because temperature has such direct effects on the fish's metabolism and level of activity. For perch in Windermere, Le Cren's (1958) correlation of annual increment with the number of degree-days above a temperature just below 14°C suggests that the perch's feeding activity depends greatly on temperature. Kempe (1962) has analysed the growth records of roach in Lake Mälären, near Stockholm, in different years. He found that the growth in the first year of life depended first on the water temperature in early June, when the eggs hatch and fry begin to feed, and then and more importantly on the tem-perature in the second half of August. If this was high, growth was greater, presumably because the growing season was extended. There is quite a good correlation between the length attained at the end of the year and the number of degree-days above 15°C. The pattern is different for adult fish but there is some correlation between annual growth increment and the number of degree-days above a temperature between 12 and 13°C, and warmth in early June again seems to be important. For a more northern lake at higher altitude there was no apparent correlation between water temperature and growth, but for fish more than two years old, growth in this lake was not nearly as good as in Lake Mälären, probably because of the lower average summer temperatures.

The growth cycles of our freshwater fishes are fairly similar, differing in whether there is any or no growth in winter and in details of the times of the year when rapid growth begins and ends. Their breeding cycles, however, are much less similar. Some fish have a breeding season which consists of only a few days – thus Hartley (1947) records the roach spawning over a few days at the end of May and beginning of June – and for most fish species there are definite periods of a few weeks during which spawning is accomplished (see Figure 15). The dace is a possible exception, for Hartley records it as spawning in June and July at Barrington, Cambridgeshire, but they spawn in the last week of February and early March in Willow Brook, Northamptonshire, and before mid-March in the Thames at Reading; one fisherman told me that they spawn twice a year in the River Mole at Cobham, Surrey.

Experiments have shown that the annual reproductive cycles of some fishes are related to and controlled by the annual cycles of temperature and light. There may be a rhythmical breeding cycle but the environmental factors determine its precise timing. For speckled trout, manipulating the light can delay or accelerate spawning; these fish normally spawn when the daylength is decreasing, and giving them artificially shortened days accelerates spawning whereas lengthening the exposure to light delays it (Figure 16). There have been very full experiments on the breeding of the three-spined stickleback (Baggerman, 1957) so I shall report these in detail.

The stickleback winters, if possible, in the sea or brackish water; during this time daylength is short and temperatures are low. As the daylength increases, gonadotropic and thyrotropic hormones are secreted, but if the water temperature stays low the thyroid does not become active. If the temperature rises in January, the thyroid becomes active and the fish begins to show a preference for fresh instead of brackish water; even if the temperature stays low, the thyroid becomes active in March as a result of increasing light and the preference for fresh water appears. The fish therefore migrate to fresh water between February and April according to temperature con-

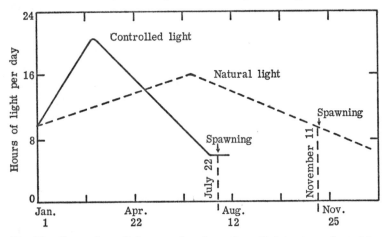

Fig. 16.—Comparison of the spawning time of speckled trout accelerated by artificially controlled light with normal spawning time under natural light. [*After Hazard and Eddy, 1951*]

ditions. The breeding season follows. Sticklebacks living in fresh waters away from the sea tend to move into deep water in winter and back to shallow water in spring.

The breeding behaviour of this fish is complicated and it has been used in many behaviour studies. At the beginning of the breeding season the male occupies a territory and defends it against other males. He then starts building a nest by digging a shallow pit into which he brings small fragments of plants which he glues together tightly with a secretion from his kidneys. When the nest is completed, it has a well-defined entrance and the male pushes his way right through. He then courts a ripe female and leads her to the nest into which she moves and lays her eggs, after which he chases her away, goes into the nest and fertilizes the eggs. They take 8 to 10 days to develop, during which time he fans them at decreasing intervals of time; he guards the young for a few days, they then disperse and the male starts to build a new nest.

The breeding season ends in the last part of June or in July, the level of thyroid secretion falls and the fish start to prefer salt water again. They migrate seawards or into deep water until the following spring. Young sticklebacks develop the preference for sea water when they are two months old or older, and may migrate in midsummer.

Sticklebacks normally breed when daylength is long and temperature is high, the season starting when daylengths are increasing and temperatures rising. Males can remain in breeding condition for 91 days in tanks and females for 60 days (during which they can lay 15 sets of eggs), provided that the daylength remains long and temperature high. After these long periods the fish stop breeding, presumably through exhaustion of gonadal products, but they begin again if the experimental conditions are maintained and they can continue to show alternation of reproductive and non-reproductive periods indefinitely, up to death. Fish in tanks with short daylength and high temperatures, however, do not mature and can be kept in this non-breeding condition for at least a year. If the daylength is increased, they rapidly come into breeding condition. Fish in tanks with short daylength and low temperatures remain in non-breeding condition; if they are suddenly exposed to high temperatures they start to breed, but the breeding period only lasts for 46 days for males and 6½ days for females unless the daylength is increased (see Table 11). Thus daylength and temperature are both important for the timing of the reproductive period and its maintenance; in experiments, sudden changes produce effects sooner than the gradual changes which are normal under natural conditions.

Young sticklebacks can be persuaded to breed when only 4 or 5 months old by exposing them to long daylength and high temperatures. They must be at least 2·2 cm long to show this effect and in nature they grow very slowly and do not attain this length until the days begin to shorten, so that they never normally come into breeding condition until they are nearly one year old. It is suggested that production of pituitary growth hormone is suppressed until the days start shortening.

Bullough (1939, 1940) found a somewhat similar situation in the minnow which breeds between May and July in the Lake District. He found that increased daylength induced early maturation but only if the water temperature exceeded a critical value of 10°C. Raising the water temperature in mid-winter, when daylength was short, had no effect on maturation. These fish breed in running water and must migrate into streams from lakes at spawning time; they move into deeper

TABLE 11. SUMMARY OF EXPERIMENTAL OBSERVATIONS ON THE STICKLEBACK (BASED ON BAGGERMAN, 1957)

Temperature	Short daylength	Long daylength
Low	Prefer salt water Non-breeding ↓	Prefer freshwater Non-breeding
High	Start spawning but stop after a short period ——————————— Do not mature———	Spawn, rest, spawn again and so on until death →Mature at once

water in winter and spend most of the time quiescent under stones, but they do take food.

Various workers have suggested critical water temperatures for the breeding of various fishes, but it seems that the same species may have different requirements according to latitude – perhaps daylength is also involved. Thus roach are quoted as requiring 7–9°C, 12°C and 16–19°C as the minimum temperature, and bream are alleged to require various temperatures between 15 and 23°C. For trout, there is some evidence that the final spawning migration depends on temperature falling, and the seaward migration of the silver eel also follows a drop in temperature.

The British freshwater fishes can be divided into three groups according to date of spawning (see Figure 15): (1) autumn and winter (late October to February); (2) spring (March to June);

(3) summer (May to July). When these are set out, as in Table 12, it is clear that the species in each category have certain features in common and differ from those of the other cate-

TABLE 12. SUMMARY OF SOME FEATURES CONNECTED WITH SPAWNING IN BRITISH FRESHWATER FISHES

Spawning season	*Autumn or winter* (*November/ February*)	*Spring* (*March/June*)	*Summer* (*May/July*)
Daylength	short, increasing *or* decreasing	increasing	long, increasing *or* decreasing
Temperature	cold (up to 10°C)	rising (10–15°C)	warm (above 16°C)
Condition of rooted plants	died down	growing	full-grown
Location of eggs:			
laid among stones	whitefishes		
in nest in gravel	salmon, trout, char	grayling	
stuck to stones		minnow, barbel, chub, loach, gudgeon, bullhead	
among weeds		perch	ruffe
stuck to weeds		pike	roach, rudd, carp, bream, tench
in nest of weeds			stickleback
Diameter of eggs	2·4 to 7 mm	1·3 to 3·2 mm	0·5 to 1·7 mm
Length of fry when ready to feed	15 to 24 mm	4 to 8 mm	2·5 mm and more
Time between laying and:			
hatching of eggs	up to 5 months	4 to 28 days	3 to 20 days
fry ready to feed	up to 6 months	3 to 7 weeks	1 to 4 weeks
Food of young fry	invertebrates (same as older fish)	diatoms, water fleas and rotifers (different from food of older fish)	

gories, although with some overlap. Important features are the size of eggs and where they are laid, the time taken to develop, and the early habits of the fry.

For all fishes, the number of eggs laid each year is related to the size of the female parent; the bigger she is, the more eggs she lays. Larger females may lay slightly larger eggs but the size of the eggs varies very little and is a characteristic of the species. Fish producing small eggs lay much larger numbers

TABLE 13. THE RELATION BETWEEN BODY LENGTH AND NUMBER
OF EGGS (NIKOLSKY, 1961)

Salmon, *Salmo salar*, eggs of diameter 5–7 mm

Body length (in cm)	50	60	70	80	90	100
Number of eggs (in thousands)		5·9	9·4	12·2	14·0	19·4

Carp, *Cyprinus carpio*, eggs of diameter 0·9–1·2 mm

Body length (in cm)	35	40	45	50	55	60	65
Number of eggs (in thousands)		181	229	375	429	550	525

than fish of the same size belonging to another species which produces large eggs (see Tables 13 and 14). The eggs always contain some yolk which is used by the developing embryos. The little fish which hatches from the egg usually still has a

TABLE 14. RELATION BETWEEN THE SIZE OF EGGS AND THE
NUMBERS PRODUCED (MAINLY AFTER SCHINDLER, 1953)

Species	Diameter of egg (mm)	Number laid per lb of female body weight
Salmon	5–7	500–1400
Trout	4–5·5	500–1200
Char	4–4·5	1400–2200
Grayling	3·2–4	3000–4500
Pike	2·5–3	10,000–20,000
Perch	2–2·5	c. 100,000
Tench	c. 1·2	c. 275,000
Carp	0·9–1·2	up to 550,000

yolk sac attached to its ventral surface and is called an alevin. When all the yolk has been consumed, the little fish must seek food for itself and it is then called a fry.

Except for the rare burbot, all the autumn and winter spawners have relatively large eggs, the summer spawners all have small eggs, and spring spawners have eggs of intermediate size. I have already discussed the implications of egg size in relation to oxygen consumption and temperature (Chapter 2).

The large eggs of salmonids give rise to large alevins and the young fry are big enough to eat the same sort of food as adults. This is almost certainly an advantage, but it must be set against the fact that each female produces relatively few eggs. Development takes a long time but the eggs laid in autumn in gravel do not hatch until spring, and the winter period of floods and perhaps snow and ice is passed within the protective, tough egg shell.

The small eggs of summer-spawning cyprinids are usually attached to water weeds. They contain little yolk and develop quickly and hatch after a few days into very small alevins. The tiny, delicate fry can eat only minute organisms such as diatoms, rotifers and water fleas, and their food is generally different from that of adults. These small food organisms are very abundant in summer in still water or in the shallow weedy areas of rivers where there is little or no flow. In some species, such as carp and bream, the fry have adhesive organs and attach themselves to plants. Since these plants are photosynthetic, there should always be plenty of oxygen in summer among these weeds. Summer spawners produce very large numbers of eggs.

Most of the spring spawners lay their eggs among or attached to stones, but perch and pike need rooted plants. The eggs are of medium size and develop in a few weeks into fry which are small and able to feed only on small organisms. Like the fry of summer spawners, these must find diatoms, rotifers and water fleas and must change their diet later to that of the adults. The fry are bigger and slightly less delicate than those of summer spawners, and the females lay relatively fewer eggs. Compared with winter spawners, these species have a possible advantage in that the eggs are laid after the difficult winter period, so there is less danger of floods and frost.

When fishes spawn there may be elaborate behaviour, including pair formation and deposition of eggs in a carefully prepared place, or the process may appear to be much more casual with large shoals composed of both sexes gathering and spawning together.

Salmonid eggs are usually laid among small stones. Female salmon and trout construct a nest (or "redd") in the gravel by "cutting" movements of the tail; they test water currents through it with the anal fin before they are ready to shed their eggs. These fish can spawn successfully only where there is suitable gravel, and if this is limited there may be much over-cutting of redds and high mortality of eggs. Redds may be exposed by winter droughts, but the female's behaviour does mean that the eggs are protected and placed so that silt does not accumulate round them.

Many spring spawners lay sticky eggs which adhere to stones and are thus protected from some hazards of stream life; those of the bullhead are guarded by the male. These fishes can breed only where there is water flowing over a stony substratum. Spawning perch form large shoals and each female lays a ribbon of eggs among the weeds and may guard them for a few hours. Pike spawn as pairs, swimming through the weeds and shedding sticky eggs among them. Most of the summer spawners, also, lay sticky eggs singly among weed beds. In some species, such as the bream, the males defend territories which may be as large as 5 square yards; the violent splashing so characteristic of these fish in the breeding season is the result of "fighting" between males. Females swim to and pair with the males in their territories and the eggs are thus spaced out among the weeds. Sticklebacks have a special spawning behaviour, as already described, and the male guards the eggs and young fry.

Territorial behaviour of spawning fish and movement of the pair while shedding eggs results in the eggs being dispersed; this is probably usually an advantage, because if the breeding season is very short, all the eggs are likely to hatch almost simultaneously and all the little fry will be competing for the same food supply. On the other hand a longer breeding season means that the eggs hatch over a longer period, and competition between them and the risk of all hatching under temporarily adverse conditions is reduced.

Among trout and salmon it is an advantage for some fry to start feeding earlier than others, for they then acquire territories earlier; in a good spawning stream, the latest fry to start to feed are likely to fail to find territories and to be forced to emigrate. The territorial system among young trout fry results in spacing them out over the bottom and sets an upper limit to the number which can survive in a given area with a given bottom structure. This has been well illustrated by some experiments in a beck in the Lake District by Le Cren (1961). He screened off five similar reaches and planted in them different numbers of alevins ranging from 3 to 234 per square yard. At the end of five months, there were about 7 fry per square yard surviving in each reach (except where the number was less to begin with) (see Figure 17). The mortality thus had

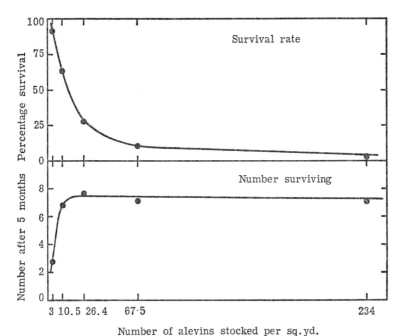

Fig. 17. The survival of brown trout fry in screened reaches of a small stream, to show that increasing the number of alevins leads to a decrease in survival rate since the number that survive per unit area is constant. [*After Le Cren, 1961*]

varied between about 97 per cent in the most densely stocked reach and 7 per cent in the least densely stocked. It became clear from this and other experiments that most of the deaths occurred between 20 and 40 days after the little trout began to feed; this is just when they are establishing territories. Fry dying from starvation were collected in the crowded sections, and growth was most rapid in the least crowded sections. The individual territories were about 4 × 4 inches for the fry.

Kalleberg (1958) found that a 9-inch trout defended 4 square yards from other fish of this size but tolerated trout of younger (smaller) classes who defended their own territories within the large one.

The young fry of cyprinids usually gather in shoals which may be very dense and include several species. These all feed on the same food organisms, which are extremely abundant in weed beds. The shoaling habit exposes many fry at once to attack by predators, but this is partly compensated for by a mutual warning reaction. Frightened minnows emit a substance from their skins which results in other minnows showing their alarm reaction. It is interesting that these alarm substances are emitted by many species of cyprinids and many of these can react to the substances emitted by members of other species – the situation is analogous to the use of similar alarm calls by different species of small birds.

Mortality may be extremely high in early life. Powan eggs in Loch Lomond are literally decimated by being eaten by adult powan which stay on the spawning grounds for two months. The caddis larva, *Phryganea*, is another important predator which ate 65 per cent of the eggs laid in one season. Probably only 5 per cent of the eggs hatch successfully in any year (see Figure 18). The territorial system among stream-living salmonids leads to heavy mortality of fry in crowded streams. For perch fry, July is a critical month in Windermere; the plankton which is their principal food decreases in amount and the little fish either eat bottom-living organisms or become cannibals and prey on smaller perch fry (Smyly, 1952). Montèn (1948) found for pike fry that the greatest relative loss was very early in their lives. These fish eat plankton and insects when small but change to fish-eating when about 10 cm long; in aquaria they become cannibals at that stage. Loch Choin, in Scotland, is of interest because the only fish species there is the pike, so these must all be cannibals as soon as they become piscivorous.

Few figures are available for other fishes, but since many of them produce large numbers of small eggs (35,000 for a roach of 18 cm length and up to 525,000 for a good-sized carp) and there are many spawners, there must be a great loss of eggs, fry or young fish. Since a good year-class (i.e. better than normal survival of fish spawned in one year) for many cyprinids is often correlated with warm sunny weather in June, this suggests that conditions when the fry begin to feed are extremely important.

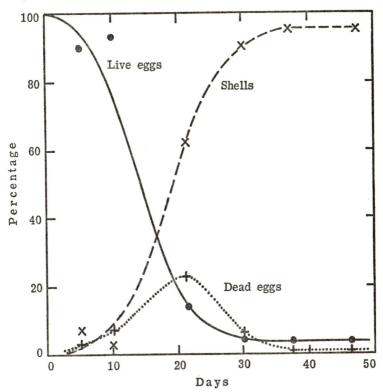

Fig. 18.—Mortality of powan eggs in Loch Lomond. The shells represent eggs attacked by larvae of the caddis *Phryganea*, which bite a hole and eat out the contents. [*After Slack*, et al., *1957*]

Table 15 shows that different species of fish mature at very different ages ranging from one year old (e.g. minnow, stone-loach, stickleback, some roach) to four years old or older (e.g. bream and some trout); the sturgeon probably is one of the oldest to mature (13 years and over). In many species the males mature when younger and smaller than the females but it is unusual to find the opposite, as perhaps in gudgeon. Fish of the same species in different waters may grow at very different rates and sometimes they mature at different ages but sometimes at the same age although of different sizes. The whole problem of the relationship between growth and maturity was discussed in detail by Alm (1959) and his conclusions are of great interest, based as they are on experimental work at the hatchery at Kalärne and on wide experience of many different species of fish in Sweden. He puts forward a general hypothesis that the faster an individual grows, the sooner will it become sexually

TABLE 15. THE ONSET OF SEXUAL MATURITY IN FRESHWATER
FISHES

	Age (*in years*) at which half the fish spawn		
	♂♂		♀♀
Minnow and stickleback		1	
Stoneloach		1 or 2	
Ruffe	1		2
Perch	1 or 2		2
Dace		2	
Tench		2 or later	
Roach	1, 2 or 3		3 or 4
Bream		3 or later	
Grayling and char	2 or 3		3 or 4
Gudgeon	3 or 4		2 or 3
Carp	3		3 or 4
Chub	3		4
Pike	3		3
Whitefishes		3 or 4	
Salmon	2 or later		4 or later
Brown trout { some waters	3		3
{ some waters	5		7
Sturgeon (R. Gironde)	14		19

mature. In any population, then, the fastest-growing individuals will mature before those that grow more slowly and those that grow most slowly will mature at the greatest age. Because spawning is an annual process, the fish with medium growth rates may actually be larger when they first spawn than those which grew faster and matured the year before. Since the gonads may eventually mature however slow the growth, slowly-growing individuals may mature when smaller than those growing faster and maturing when younger. This is illustrated in Figure 19A.

The onset of maturity is also determined genetically, at least in some fishes, for instance, brown trout. Alm compared two races of trout, one from a small stream, where they grow slowly and males mature at three years old, and the other from a large lake, where they grow fast and males mature when five years old. In hatchery ponds, fish from both sources grew at identical rates, but the male river trout spawned when about

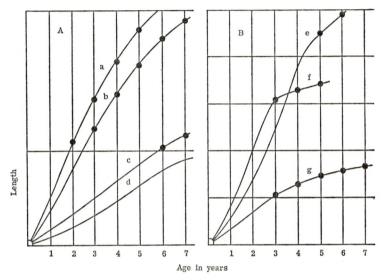

Fig. 19.—Diagrams to show the relationship between sexual maturity, size and age in fishes. (The points indicate that the fish spawn that year.) A—maturity is attained when the fish reach a threshold length, represented by the horizontal line: a, b, c and d are growth curves of fish growing at very different rates and therefore becoming mature at different ages (2, 3, 6 and more than 7 years old, respectively). B—maturity is genetically determined and occurs when the fish reaches a given age, depending on its race; curve e, fast-growing and late-maturing; curve f, fast-growing and early-maturing; curve g, slow-growing and early-maturing. [*Based on Alm, 1959*]

3 years old and the male lake trout not until two years later. As in natural conditions, the lake trout were very much larger at their onset of maturity than the river trout. In each population the faster-growing fish spawned earlier, but the threshold of size at which they began to spawn was genetically determined and was much larger for one population than for the other (see Figure 19B). This arrangement may seem odd but is well adapted to the conditions under which trout live. As trout

grow larger they produce more eggs, and the eggs of larger fish are usually larger than those of smaller ones. If trout of different sizes spawn in a river, then there is a slightly greater probability of fish from larger eggs surviving than those from smaller ones, and if there is a chance mortality, affecting all equally, then more offspring will probably survive from the larger fish than from the smaller ones. If size at maturity is inherited, the offspring of larger fish, which survive better, will pass on their pattern of maturity to their offspring and it will be selected as the pattern for the river. If the trout live under conditions where growth is slow, then they will take many years to reach the threshold of maturity if this is set at a large size. Many may well die before achieving the size limit, but if any fish spawn before they reach this size they will leave some offspring. Thus the threshold for maturity is likely to be set, by natural selection, for a size which can be achieved within the normal lifespan; slow growth but early maturity at small size is the pattern for many trout waters. Yet another form of life pattern is shown by trout which are selected for rapid growth but early maturity, for instance under hatchery conditions. These will spawn at a smaller size than the long-lived fast-growing trout of some natural waters but will be much larger than the short-lived, early-maturing, slow-growing trout of other natural waters.

Growth rate is determined largely by environment, and trout from different natural waters grow at identical rates if kept under identical conditions. The growth rates of fishes are very plastic; they normally fall off as the fish grow older, but many fishes can continue to grow in length throughout their lives and stunted fishes can show spurts of growth if transferred to better conditions at any stage of their lives. Perch and roach from waters where they normally grow slowly and mature late show increased growth when transferred to waters with better conditions for growth and they then achieve the limiting size and mature at a younger age. There is some indication that a long hot summer results in more perch becoming mature the following year at a size slightly smaller than normal.

Alm also discussed whether maturity affects the growth rate and longevity of fishes. He concluded from his experiments that fish which grow fast and mature when young continue to grow well and remain larger than others in the same ponds which grow more slowly and therefore mature later. He also concluded that early or late maturity has no relevance to longevity. Males usually mature when younger and smaller than females but their average lifespan is the same.

However, among British trout there seem to be some which show a greater effect of maturity than do others. In trout selected for fast early growth with maturity at 3 years old (at a length of about 25 cm) the subsequent annual increments fall off markedly; these trout seem to convert more of their food intake into gonadal products and less into body growth than others which do not grow quite so fast to begin with, mature when older and perhaps larger (30 cm or more) and keep growing well after this (compare curves e and f in Figure 19B).

Alm's experimental fishes lived under good conditions in a hatchery and were provided with food. The salmonids were stripped of their milt and eggs; they thus did not have to seek their food, did not have to adapt their feeding to foods available in the changing seasons and, above all, did not have to seek spawning grounds and take part in the arduous activities of spawning. Under natural conditions, the effort of spawning involves great expenditure of energy and exposes the fish to many hazards. In trout populations where nearly all the fish mature at the same age, a marked decrease in average growth rate occurs in the years following maturity; where the onset of maturity in the population is spread over several years, this is not obvious. Many trout in Alm's hatchery lived for 10 years, whether they began to spawn at 3 or at 4 or even at 7 years old, but wild trout which spawn at 3 years old seldom live to be more than 6 or 7 years old. Trout which mature when older may live much longer (see Figure 20). Some large late-maturing trout seem to spawn only in alternate years.

It is a common finding among perch and wild cyprinid fishes that all the older and larger fishes are females. The males mature earlier and seem to die when younger. The juvenile sex ratio is usually 1 : 1, but the population of large fish may consist of 80 per cent or 90 per cent females whereas in collections of spawning fish there may be 80 per cent of males. Since the males usually spend longer in the spawning areas and may indulge in energetic territorial behaviour, they must be subject to greater physiological stress and to greater hazards from

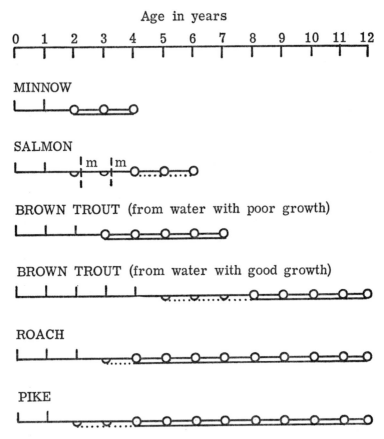

Fig. 20.—Diagram to illustrate the different types of life histories found among British freshwater fishes. Full circles indicate years when the majority of individuals spawn; half circles indicate that the majority of males spawn. Double lines mean that more than half the population of that age is mature; dots below the single line mean that more than half the male fishes of that age are mature. In the salmon life history the vertical dashed lines with *m* beside them indicate when the smolts migrate to the sea, and the half circles before these indicate that many male salmon parr become ripe before migration; the majority of salmon which return and spawn in fresh water die soon afterwards, but the time spent in the sea varies.

predators than females and it is not surprising that they die when younger. In the sheltered conditions of the hatchery, they survive much better. Alm records four perch which had probably lived for 27 or 28 years in his hatchery; these were one male of 35 cm and three females of 27, 29 and 38 cm length. The sex ratio regularly remained approximately 1 : 1 in his perch ponds after 9 or more years.

Species of fishes differ greatly in their size range. Thus, most minnows, loaches and sticklebacks are less than 10 cm long but carp and bream grow to several times this length. There may be a "limiting size" for many species; thus roach are very unlikely to exceed 40 cm, pike in Windermere seem to grow towards an ultimate length of 100 cm, carp in the Amur River to 90 cm and bream in the Aral Sea to 45 cm. For brown trout in Britain there is no single limiting length, since "good fish" for different waters may vary from ½ lb to more than 20 lb. This is a highly plastic species and perhaps fish which are more conservative in diet and habitat are less variable in limiting size.

The natural span of life may vary between sexes and from water to water (see Figure 20). Small fishes such as the minnow, the stoneloach and the stickleback may live for only 3 to 5 years, whereas cyprinids such as the roach commonly live for more than 10 years; indeed in some parts of the Thames these fish do not attain the "legal size" until that age. Two large pike from Windermere were 14 years old (weight 32¼ and 35¼ lb). Salmon may spend two years in fresh water and then three years in the sea and reach this sort of weight when only 5 years old, whereas sea-trout grow much more slowly, spawn more often and are commonly much older.

We know very little really about why fish die. There is generally a heavy mortality in early stages – usually, perhaps always, as a result of competition for food. Where predatory fish such as pike are present, these must consume large numbers of other fish. Parasites presumably take their toll. The best-documented cases are the infections with plerocercoids of *Diphyllobothrium* spp. which have killed large numbers of trout in Malham Tarn (Holmes, 1960) and in certain reservoirs (Hickey and Harris, 1947) at 4½ years old. Kempe (1962) quoted a roach population in Sweden where a quarter of the two-year-old fish were infected with the tapeworm *Ligula*; he expected the majority of these to be killed as a result. Older fish have more time to accumulate parasites, and probably death from parasitic infection becomes more likely with increased age, whereas death from attack by predatory fish becomes less likely as size and age increase. Birds and mammals may be important predators and are best excluded from commercially important fisheries. They also harbour the adult stages of many parasites dangerous to fish, such as *Diphyllobothrium* and *Ligula,* and if they are kept away, these parasites cannot get back to the water. Anglers, of course, also take their toll. They should be the most important predators on edible fish.

When the lifespan is short, juveniles form a high proportion of the population (see Figure 20) and probably the variation in survival of juveniles in different years is not very marked. This sort of population can recover quickly from sudden catastrophic depletion of numbers. If the lifespan is long, and adult fish spawn many times, the proportion of juveniles is low and most of the population consists of adults. These produce very great numbers of eggs but survival of fry is usually very poor. Occasional year-classes are markedly successful and dominate the population for many years. This type of life cycle seems to be adapted to stable conditions for adult fish, and consequent good survival of these, but very hazardous conditions in early life. When these conditions happen to be advantageous, many young survive and form a good year-class. This must happen at least every five to ten years or the adult population would decline through natural mortality and lack of recruitment. Very dense populations develop in some waters and the individuals are then stunted and slow-growing.

How does the distribution of fishes seem to be related to their life histories? Our autumn spawners are salmonids, primarily migratory fish spending part of their lives in the sea or in lakes. These lay their eggs in swift streams where there are few other fishes to prey on them. Perhaps the adult fish have a better chance of returning to the sea to feed and surviving to spawn again if they spawn in autumn and are able to move downstream with the winter floods. River levels tend to rise in autumn and this enables large spawning fish such as salmon to penetrate into small streams which they could not enter in low water conditions in summer.

Salmonid eggs are less tolerant of high temperatures than are the adult fish, and the main difficulty in establishing trout populations in the tropics is usually that of finding suitable conditions of temperature and substratum for successful spawning. Each adult produces relatively few eggs but these are protected by being laid in gravel and the fry do not emerge from the gravel until after the winter floods. These fry are sufficiently powerful swimmers to head a fast current from the time they begin to feed. There is no critical transition stage when fry have to change their feeding habits to adopt an adult type of food; the critical stage is early in fry life when they establish their territories.

These salmonid fishes are certainly well adapted to live in waters where rooted vegetation is of little importance. Thus they can live in more arctic conditions, in more barren waters, and in more remote places than cyprinids. As they grow larger, they can forage downstream and out to sea but must return to headstreams to spawn.

The lifespan of freshwater fishes is usually between five and ten years. Among spring and summer spawners there is the distinction between small fishes with short life histories, which usually lay their eggs among stones and sand in running water, and the larger fishes with long lifespans which usually lay their eggs among plants. The former species usually produce rather small numbers of eggs per individual. They tend to live in fast water where the dangers of floods and droughts are quite considerable, and the population structure, with a high proportion of juveniles, is adapted to quick re-establishment after such disasters. They breed in spring, so the overwintering phase involves maturing and mature fish instead of the developing eggs. The eggs are laid after the spring floods and development is very rapid and results in small fry whose food is at first different from that of the adults.

The species of fish spawning among weeds are limited by this habit to spawning in early or late summer and must therefore overwinter as adults. Our species are typically long-lived and each female lays many eggs and spawns many times. The average annual recruitment is very low but occasional year-classes are successful; some weather factors affecting food supplies may perhaps account for the good survival in these years. Normally there must be competition between the many individuals of many species which all seek the same sort of food at almost the same time, and there is probably also heavy predation on these shoals of fry. Submerged plants in summer release more oxygen into the water than they consume, so there should always be plenty of this in the water where the eggs are laid and the young fry seek their food.

The eurythermal cyprinid fishes, with low adult requirements for oxygen, could, in theory, live in any water but they are unable to breed in fast streams or where there are few plants, e.g. in rocky lakes; they must find plenty of rooted, submerged plants among which their fry can feed. The very tolerant adults cannot penetrate far up rivers because their physical stamina is not sufficient to cope with the current. Coldwater fishes, on the other hand, must find gravel and preferably flowing water for spawning, but older fish can penetrate down rivers and into productive lakes if oxygen and temperature conditions allow. Species with intermediate degrees of tolerance, such as chub, are probably limited in distribution by their need to find stones for spawning near sheltered water, with many small organisms on which their fry can feed.

Chapter 5

The feeding of
freshwater fishes

A NIMALS are limited in their geographical distribution: first, by their means of dispersal and the barriers which prevent or retard this; then, by their physiological potentialities, which enable them to tolerate only certain ranges of physico-chemical factors in the environment, such as temperature and oxygen concentration; and lastly, by the effect of biotic factors, that is, of the other living organisms in the environment. One of the most important ways in which animals affect each other is through their food supplies, and I shall discuss here the feeding of our freshwater fishes and consider how far their distribution is limited by their diets and feeding methods and by possible competition between species for the same food supply.

"All flesh is grass" is a pithy summary of the fact that almost all the energy used by living organisms on this earth comes ultimately from the sun. Green plants use the energy of sunlight in the process of photosynthesis and build up organic compounds such as sugars and amino-acids from carbon dioxide, water and mineral salts. They can then use the amino-acids and sugars for growth, for production of energy (by the process of respiration), or for storage. Animals are capable only of limited synthesis of the simpler organic compounds but they can use them to build up very complex substances such as proteins; they must obtain the simpler compounds from other organisms. Biochemists have found, for instance, that chinook salmon require the same amino-acids in the diet as rats and are therefore less versatile than man who is able to synthesize two of these (but must be provided with the other eight). All animals obtain energy by the process of respiration in which they break down organic compounds, usually sugars, to produce carbon dioxide and water; all these compounds come eventually from plants. There is thus a transfer of energy from plants to animals in the form of organic compounds which the animal

uses for growth as well as for respiration. If the energy coming
originally from sunlight is traced through a community of
organisms, a diagram can be constructed which is the same as
the "food web" showing which species of organism prey on
which or eat which sort of food. A generalized food web is
shown in Figure 21.

In fresh waters, the plants are either microscopic algae (e.g.
diatoms) or flowering plants (and a few mosses and ferns), and
the animals cover a great size range from the single-celled
microscopic Protozoa to large fishes through a variety of
invertebrate animals such as worms, crustaceans, insects and
molluscs. Curiously few of these animals in Britain feed wholly

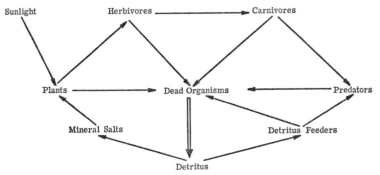

Fig. 21.—A food web, with the arrows indicating the directions of energy flow.

and directly on the plants and Hynes (1963) has recently
suggested that *detritus*, in the form of decaying leaves falling
from trees growing beside the river, is the real basis of the food
web in British fresh waters. The situation is different in the
tropics, where there are many species of animals, including
fishes, feeding entirely on plants – and where there is no regular
or considerable leaf-fall. Hynes argues that our aquatic flowering
plants have recently colonized fresh waters from marshes – it
will be interesting to see how his ideas stand up to the test of
time. Our fishes include some strict carnivores but most are
omnivores. Our freshwater invertebrates are often omnivores.
Percival and Whitehead (1929) found only 10 per cent of
species to be carnivorous in the Yorkshire streams they studied.
Worms (annelids) are mostly detritus feeders; crustaceans may
be carnivores (some water fleas and the crayfish, *Astacus*), but

many eat detritus (the shrimp, *Gammarus*, and the slater, *Asellus*); insects – the most numerous in species of all aquatic animals – include herbivores, detritus feeders and carnivores. The food chains in fresh waters often have few links. Thus Hartley (1948) observed the following chains in the River Cam at Barrington:

Date	Plant or detritus	Eaten by herbivore	Eaten by carnivore	Eaten by carnivore
31 March 1939	*Spirogyra* filaments	gudgeon	pike	
27 May 1939	Plant fragments	stickleback	pike	
14 March 1940	Diatoms	*Simulium* (reed smut) larvae	bullhead	
18 July 1940	Plant fragments and diatoms	*Simulium* larvae	dace	
2 June 1940		mayfly and caddis larvae	loach	eel
7 October 1939		mayfly nymphs and *Simulium* larvae	minnow	pike

As the energy is passed through a food web, some is dissipated at each transfer. This is because all organisms must use energy for living; this is not very obvious from casual observation of plants, but most animals move from place to place and collect their food actively and all this entails the output of energy. The energy required simply to maintain life by an inactive animal is its basal metabolic rate. This varies with temperature, especially in a poikilotherm, and increases as the temperature is raised. A normal animal moves about, at least part of the time, and its food must be used to satisfy the energy required for this activity as well as for basal metabolism. Thus all animals have a "maintenance requirement" which includes food used for normal activity as well as for basal metabolism. Activity may vary greatly with temperature, so the maintenance requirement curve may be quite different from that for the basal metabolic rate (see Figure 6). An animal can grow only if it eats more food than is required for maintenance. Even so, it cannot convert 100 per cent of the extra food intake into its own flesh. The structural and other proteins of different species are different in detail and there must be some re-arrangement of the constituents of the ingested food, to make the characteristic proteins. Probably the least amount of change is involved when one fish eats another and it is interesting that pike eating trout can convert 50 per cent of the ingested food (after allowing for maintenance) into new pike flesh. For trout eating meat (or *Gammarus*) the conversion is of the order of 20 to 25 per cent, and for fish eating plants the conversion is 10 to 15 per cent. Plant proteins differ markedly from animal proteins, so herbivores have to re-arrange the components of their food a great deal and normally find themselves with more waste to eliminate than do carnivores.

Elton (1927) pointed out that the numbers of herbivores are usually much greater than those of the carnivores that prey upon them; thus he set up the concept of the pyramid of numbers. Sufficient herbivores must survive to reproduce and maintain their numbers. The loss of energy at each transfer means that the biomass of herbivores consumed must be greater than that of the carnivores preying on them. It is thus not surprising that omnivores, herbivores and detritus feeders together should greatly outnumber carnivores in fresh waters. Parasites are a special class of carnivores; they continue the pyramid by having a smaller biomass than their hosts but they often greatly outnumber them.

In a simple food chain, a change in numbers of one category has characteristic effects on other categories such that the numbers of alternate links in the chain become more and less numerous. Thus, in Figure 21, if the carnivores increase, there will be a decrease in the numbers of herbivores and an increase in the biomass of surviving plants. Probably this will be followed by an increase in the numbers of "predators" and these will reduce the numbers of carnivores; the numbers of herbivores will then increase and the amount of plant food will decrease. Thus there may be regular fluctuations in numbers, unless any one category becomes so numerous that it eats out its food supply, leading to catastrophic results. Since food webs in fresh waters are complex, with many omnivores, it is not possible to detect this sort of effect.

Let us consider the characteristics of freshwater fishes using different types of food. Carnivores such as the trout and salmon see their prey and chase it. They swim swiftly with excellent control of turning, so they can chase prey seen at a wide angle to the body axis. When they are young they depend entirely on food drifting into their field of vision, and trout eat a great deal of midwater food throughout their lives, although they soon learn to recognize and eat animals on the bottom. The pike is a quite different sort of carnivore; it lurks almost motionless until it sees prey, or senses movement through its lateral line, then manoeuvres itself round until its snout points at the prey, and finally, with a swift movement of the tail, darts forward – literally like an arrow – and seizes the fish (or other food). If the prey is a trout and notices the pike, it has a good chance of escape because it can change course quickly and the pike cannot. I have kept young pike and slightly smaller rainbow trout together in an aquarium but had to separate them because the pike were rendered so "nervous" by the circling movements of the trout. Sometimes predatory fish locate their victims by other senses than sight but we have none of these specialized fish in Britain.

Carnivores may have to use much energy in catching their food. All that they eat, however, is first-class protein and when the food is fish there is very little waste; when insects, crustaceans and molluscs are eaten a good deal of indigestible matter is of course taken in with the digestible flesh. Carnivorous fishes usually swallow whole animals into a stomach which is a bag that holds the food and in which digestion may begin by the secretion of acid and pepsin (see Figure 22). The rest of the gut is usually short and often there are pyloric caeca at the beginning of the intestine (these increase the intestinal area and perhaps allow much alkaline secretion which will neutralize the acid from the stomach). Carnivores characteristically swallow their prey whole and feed to repletion and then rest before feeding again, so there are periods when they are "off the feed", and their stomachs are often empty when caught.

Because the contents of plant cells cannot be digested until their walls are broken, fishes eating plants must be able to break cellulose and wood cells mechanically; i.e. they have some method of chewing up the food. Most of our plant-eating fish are cyprinids and these have pharyngeal teeth at the back end of the gill region. The number and shape of these teeth are, in fact, diagnostic of the different species and presumably allow for the chewing of foods of different size and degrees of hardness (see Figure 23). Herbivorous fish have to eat relatively more than carnivores because much plant material is unusable roughage, so they usually feed throughout the day and the gut lacks a stomach. The intestine is long; it may be up to fifteen times as long as the fish and digestion proceeds gradually all

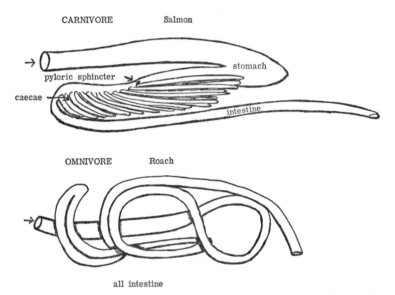

Fig. 22.—Comparison of the guts of the salmon, a carnivorous fish, and the roach, an omnivorous fish.

the way along it. It is coiled so that it fits into the body cavity and there are no pyloric caeca. Sometimes the liver is dispersed among the coils of the gut, instead of being a discrete organ at the front end of the body cavity as it is in most vertebrate animals. Herbivores do not have to chase mobile food but they must chew it up and must ingest more and waste more than do carnivores living entirely on animals. They are often deep-bodied and swim slowly.

Detritus feeders are also faced with a food supply which does not move but it is amorphous and usually dispersed among deposits of mud or earth. Their usual habit is to suck up

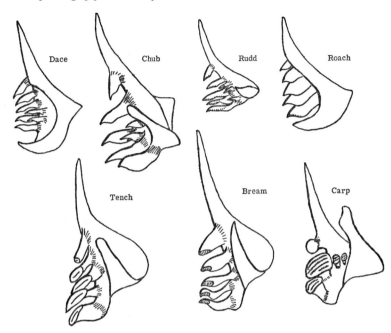

Fig. 23.—Pharyngeal teeth of seven species of British cyprinids. The pharyngeal bone with teeth attached is that from the right side and is viewed from above. Dace are insectivorous, chub piscivorous and the others omnivours. Tench, bream and carp chew up their food into small pieces, the others tear up the food. The teeth work against a hard pad in the upper wall of the pharynx; their number and arrangement are useful diagnostic characters. [*After Torbett, 1961*]

Fig. 24.—Carp with mouth closed and open.

Depth in centimetres

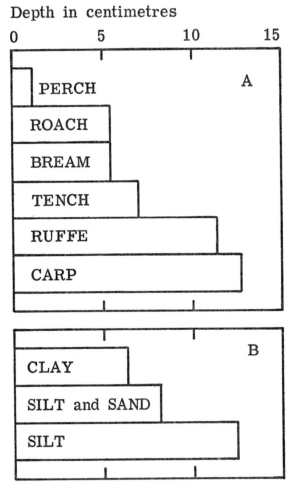

Fig. 25.—The depth of penetration into the bottom by feeding fishes. A—comparison of the depth probed by different species of fish. B—comparison of the depth probed by carp in different types of substratum. [*After Nikolsky, 1961*]

bottom deposits, grind them between pharyngeal teeth, swallow them and digest what is usable, egesting the rest. They are likely to eat much unusable material, so they feed continuously and, like herbivores, lack a stomach but have a very long intestine. The sucking mouth is their characteristic feature (Figure 24) and they are usually well provided with taste and tactile organs, often on barbels, close to the mouth. The probing action of different fishes is compared in Figure 25. Bottom deposits containing detritus usually contain many invertebrate detritus feeders, especially chironomid larvae, so fishes feeding on these deposits are actually omnivores which ingest a fair amount of animal food.

When fishes feed on very small organisms, be these plants or animals, they need methods of concentrating them out of the water; usually their gill-rakers are elongated to form a sieve,

TABLE 16. THE FOOD OF FISH IN THE RIVER CAM AND SHEPRETH BROOK, 1939–1941

The occurrence of food of each category is expressed for each species as percentages of the total occurrence of foods (i.e. total fish containing foods) of all categories (Hartley, 1948)

	Fish	Molluscs	Insects	Crustaceans	Weeds and algal filaments	Diatoms	Others
Pike	85	—	9	6	—	—	—
Brown trout	13	7	48	21	3	$1\frac{1}{2}$	$6\frac{1}{2}$
Eel	19	5	24	44	5	—	3
Gudgeon	—	12	57	24	6	+	1
Bullhead	—	1	58	39	—	—	2
Stickleback	—	2	51	24	14	8	1
Perch*	10	—	30	60	—	—	—
Loach*	—	—	65	35	—	—	—
Roach	—	19	36	7	30	7	1
Dace	—	9	53	6	22	10	—
Minnow	—	—	43	9	21	23	4

* Very few specimens

as in whitefishes. Feeding on microscopic organisms is worth while only if they are very abundant, because a large fish must eat enormous numbers to obtain even its maintenance requirement. In fresh waters plankton is dense only in lakes, so plankton-feeding fish are characteristic of still waters. Trout feed on planktonic animals by the laborious method of picking them out individually and swallowing them. Even so, a $\frac{3}{4}$-lb trout may find it worth while to eat zooplankton in midsummer in a rich lake such as Lough Derg.

Many young fishes eat plankton or live on the rotifers and water fleas among plants in rivers or lakes, or on ostracods,

TABLE 17. THE ANIMAL FOODS FOUND MOST FREQUENTLY IN FISH FROM THE RIVER CAM AND SHEPRETH BROOK, 1939–41. For each species of fish, the number of fish in which each food occurred is expressed as a percentage of the total number of fish examined (Hartley, 1948)

Fish	Ephemeropteran (mayfly) nymphs	Trichopteran (caddis) larvae	Adult beetles	Simulium (reed smut) larvae	Chironomid larvae	Gammarus and Astacus (crustaceans)	Copepoda and Chydorus (water fleas)
Pike	73	—	—	—	—	—	—	—
Brown trout	$26\frac{1}{2}$	$26\frac{1}{2}$	84	43	—	—	33 + 10	—
Eel	22	$13\frac{1}{2}$	—	—	$5\frac{1}{2}$	—	31 + 26	—
Gudgeon	—	8	6	—	9	61	18	$8\frac{1}{2} + 7\frac{1}{2}$
Bullhead	—	11	13	—	—	$21\frac{1}{2}$	$40\frac{1}{2}$	—
Stickleback	—	9	—	—	—	42	—	24 + 6
Roach	—	—	—	—	6	$14\frac{1}{2}$	$8\frac{1}{2}$	—
Dace	—	—	30	8	8	12	$5\frac{1}{2}$	—
Minnow	—	—	—	—	—	$26\frac{1}{2}$	—	—

often numerous in the deposits in shallow parts of rivers; the size discrepancy is much less and the little fishes, like the trout, pick up the organisms individually. However, if yearling pike are fed only on plankton they gradually cease to grow and eventually die.

In practice many of our freshwater fishes are omnivorous, taking both animal and plant food, the proportions varying with age and environmental conditions. There have been few studies of how the available food is shared among a community of fishes and the most complete was by Hartley (1948) who observed the fish living in the Shepreth Brook and the River Cam at Barrington. On the basis of the information in Table 16 he divided them into the following categories:

1. specialized fish-eater – pike.
2. unspecialized carnivores – trout and eel, the former being remarkable for the wide range of food species consumed.
3. carnivores eating mainly insects and crustaceans – gudgeon, stickleback, bullhead. The loach and perch also fitted into this category but were not very common.
4. omnivores eating mainly insects and plants – roach, dace and minnows. The plants were usually filamentous algae which are present in enormous quantities in summer but in much smaller amount in winter.

Clearly there must be competition for food between many of these species of fish since insects, for instance, are eaten by all except the pike, and even these eat insects and crustaceans, when they are small before they take to fish-eating. However, in spite of considerable overlap no two species ate exactly the same proportion of food, as is illustrated by Table 17.

Chironomid larvae were the preferred food of gudgeon, sticklebacks and minnows and were also eaten by many roach, dace and bullheads, but they were not eaten by trout. *Simulium* larvae were eaten by many gudgeon, dace and roach; caddises were the preferred food of dace and of the brown trout and were eaten also by gudgeon and bullheads. Hartley concluded that "the differences between the food requirements of one species and another lie in the different inroads which they make upon the components of a common stock. As the supply of one food becomes more abundant, and of another scarce, so the balance of competition between one species and another will be altered. . . . the degree of general competition is such that few of the members of the fish fauna will be wholly unaffected by an enforced change in the diet of some other species".

Certainly the trout, for which a great deal of information has been collected, appears to feed on the animals most readily available to it. When there is a "hatch of fly" (i.e. emergence of adults of mayflies, stoneflies, caddises and midges) trout will stuff themselves on these, but on other occasions they may fill themselves with *Simulium* larvae or else take a mixture of the shrimps, mayfly nymphs, caddis larvae, etc. that may be

TABLE 18. COMPARISON OF THE DIETS OF COMMON AND SILVER BREAM— MEAN LENGTHS (IN CM) OF FISH CONTAINING DIFFERENT ITEMS OF FOOD (HARTLEY, 1947)

| | | *Mean length of fish containing:* | | | |
	Mean length of whole sample	Diatoms	Weeds and algal filaments	Crustaceans	Insects	Molluscs
White bream	12·34	—	12·47	11·6	13·0	13·25
Common bream						
1939	17·26	14·25	18·95	15·44	21·1	24·6
1940	16·15	11·57	16·79	15·01	18·98	20·9

moving among the stones and plants. They feed on terrestrial insects when these fall on to the water surface. This adaptability should ensure efficient utilization of any food resource which becomes abundant but trout are limited by the need to see their food moving, whereas fishes grubbing on the bottom may tap a food supply (e.g. chironomid larvae) that is invisible and therefore useless to trout.

It is a rule accepted by many ecologists that "two closely related species never fill exactly the same niche", and this is usually interpreted as "they never eat exactly the same food"; but Hartley (1947) recorded just this type of competition between white bream and common bream in the slow muddy waters of the Old West River in Cambridgeshire, the Grantham Canal, the lower Cam and Reach Lode. Both species show a marked change in diet with change in size (Table 18), from diatoms (when small) through crustaceans and plants and then insects with molluscs included in the diet of the large fish. Bream have pharyngeal teeth, so the food is greatly chewed up and often difficult to identify. Common bream grow larger and the diet changes at larger sizes than for the white bream.

The perch and the ruffe are another pair of related fishes with rather similar diets (see Table 19), also changing as the fish grow, but the latter probe better and eat chironomid larvae more than the former and do not eat fish, which are a good food for larger perch.

The roach is an omnivorous fish with diverse feeding habits but usually eats more vegetable than animal food. The younger

TABLE 19. COMPARISON OF THE DIETS OF PERCH (LESS THAN 14 CM LONG) AND RUFFE

Occurrences of different foods as percentages of total occurrences
(Hartley, 1947)

	Fish	*Molluscs*	*Insects*	*Crustaceans*	*Plants*	*Diatoms*
Norfolk Broads						
Perch (34)	8	—	46	46	—	—
Ruffe (198)	—	1	73	16	9	1
Old West River						
Perch (24)	9	—	52	35	4	—
Ruffe (6)	—	—	60	40	—	—

Number of specimens examined in brackets

fish eat planktonic crustaceans and diatoms; insects, flowering plants and algae increase in importance as the fish grow larger, while molluscs are a food of the older fish. However, roach grow at very different rates in different waters and it has been suggested that growth is most rapid where the proportion of animal food in the diet is greatest. This is illustrated by Table 20. Kempe (1962) has summarized many comments on this subject. He himself found that roach grew faster on a predominantly vegetable diet in Lake Mälaren than they did on a mainly animal diet in Lake Sarnasjön, but he ascribed the differences in growth rate to differences in temperature. It seems clear that all over Europe the young roach during their first year eat microscopic plants and animals, found in the plankton, among plants or near the bottom. Thereafter they

TABLE 20. THE DIETS OF ROACH FROM THREE LOCALITIES AND THEIR AVERAGE LENGTHS FOR THE FIRST FIVE YEARS OF LIFE (FROM HARTLEY, 1947)

	Occurrences of different foods as percentages of total occurrences					Length (in cm)* at end of year				
	Molluscs	Insects	Crustaceans	Plants and algae	Diatoms	I	II	III	IV	V
Norfolk Broads	4½	4½	14	56½	20	6·9	9·3	11·2	12·7	13·7
Old West River	11	10	17½	50½	11	6·6	9·3	11·2	12·5	14·2
R. Cam (Barrington)	21	38	5	31½	3	7·0	10·6	13·0	16·2	18·2

* From scale reading

eat increasing quantities of filamentous algae and possibly zooplankton as well. When 10 to 12 cm long, they begin to eat more bottom fauna including chironomid larvae, shrimp and caddises and also detritus; from 15 cm they will eat molluscs. It seems that roach which grow big and live in lakes *always* eat molluscs.

Most cyprinids show a change in diet as they grow older. The young fry eat diatoms and small animals such as water fleas and rotifers; they may soon start eating filamentous algae and so progress gradually to the adult diets of mixed plant and animal foods in various proportions. They are, in fact, feeding when young on organisms living among plants, swimming in mid-water or moving actively over the substratum, and they gradually develop the habit of grubbing in deposits or chewing up mouthfuls of weed and molluscs. The change in diet is accompanied by changes in the pharyngeal teeth and in the gut. These fish start by eating the most easily seen foods and then progress to foods which are more difficult to digest and require specializations of mouth, teeth and gut. There must be greater competition between fry than among the older fishes, and it is presumably because the fry are feeding on a food which is temporarily very abundant that many are able to survive in spite of the competition between them.

Two species of British fishes – the perch and the roach – are prone to over-populate waters. Stunted populations of both of these are well known and the reduction of numbers present in lakes has resulted in better growth. The perch is insectivorous until it reaches a limiting size after which it begins to eat fish; where the young cannot find enough food for rapid growth, fish-eating is either never attained, or only occasionally, giving the phenomenon of the rare "specimen" fish among a vast collection of "tiddlers". For roach the critical stage seems to be the transition to mollusc-eating which tends to occur at about 15 cm. Again, some populations may contain 99·9 per cent of small, stunted individuals and 0·1 per cent large fish. It is the degree of competition among the young and small fish which determines whether the old fish will be large or small.

Salmonid fry eat the same food organisms as older individuals, except that they cannot eat fish or large crustaceans; thus they may compete with the older fish. Because of the territorial

system trout and salmon fry and the older fish are spaced out
over the bottom, with several small fish living in their small
territories within the large territory of an older trout. They all
feed on organisms drifting to them with the current – the fry
rely exclusively on this "living drift" to begin with, but larger
fish take organisms moving on the bottom or near the surface
as well. The territorial habit limits the number of trout of
different sizes that can live in a stream, and must assist in
sharing out the available food supply, but some territories will
be better placed and their occupants will obtain more food and
grow faster than the rest. Salmonid fish in lakes are probably
not territorial.

The fauna and flora of lakes and rivers vary greatly but are
much affected by the depth and flow of the water and the type
of substratum (see pp. 59 to 62). Small swift streams contain
mainly carnivorous fish – trout and salmon parr, bullhead,
minnow. Large slow rivers have mixed communities mainly of
omnivorous fish such as the bottom-feeding bream, the weed-
living roach and the midwater-feeding rudd, but the predatory
pike is common, too. Intermediate types of river have mixed
communities, with the piscivorous chub and insectivorous dace
in the more rapid and roach in the less rapid parts, and the
carnivorous perch, loach and gudgeon frequently present.
The River Cam at Barrington is an example of a river with this
type of mixed community.

Among lakes, the deep unproductive mountain lakes are
typically salmonid waters and the trout, char and whitefish in
them are all carnivores. The basic plants are the desmids and
diatoms of the phytoplankton and a few higher plants grow
round the shore, but the extent of the shallow water is usually
much less than that of deep water. Char feed predominantly
on zooplankton and trout on the bottom fauna and food of
terrestrial origin, whilst larger trout become piscivorous.
Lakes which are slightly more productive usually support perch
and pike as well as the salmonids; these fish, too, are carnivores,
the perch being fairly similar in diet to trout and the pike becoming a specialized piscivore after reaching 10 cm in length.
Small fish are often present and these again are mainly
carnivorous. The way the food is shared among the fish species
in Windermere is illustrated in Table 21.

The more productive lakes are usually fairly shallow, lie in rich agricultural country and may have much weed growth, both submerged and emergent, while the bottom is usually of soft mud. Hence the bottom fauna consists largely of burrowing animals available only to fish with sucking mouths. There may be a rich plankton and the plants may carry a rich growth of algae and shelter dense colonies of weed-living water fleas and rotifers. The fish species are mainly cyprinids and many of these are omnivorous. Such fish as tench, carp and bream suck up the bottom mud, digest the detritus and animals in it, and then egest the inorganic particles. Pike may do well in such lakes,

TABLE 21. FOOD RELATIONSHIPS OF THE FISH IN WINDERMERE
(FROST AND BROWN, 1967)

Food organisms	*Fish feeding on these organisms*
Planktonic crustaceans	Char, young perch, young pike, minnow, stickleback
	trout (occasionally)
Larval aquatic insects	Trout, perch, eel, bullhead
	char (rarely)
Molluscs	Trout, eel
Bottom-living crustaceans	Trout, perch, bullhead
	char (to a small extent)
Attached algae	Minnow
Fish	Larger trout, larger perch, pike

where there are many fish as food for them; roach are often present in very great numbers and rudd may also occur.

Trout introduced into such waters may grow very well if no other species of fish are present but they appear to be unable to survive if there are many cyprinids, perhaps because the latter stir up the bottom. The oxygen regime of these lakes also favours fish which can survive low concentrations of dissolved oxygen, since a thermocline is usually established in early summer and the hypolimnion soon becomes devoid of oxygen.

The food supply available for fishes varies throughout the year. In summer the growth of plants, both large and small, is luxuriant but there is a shortage of living plant food in winter, when many macrophytes have died down and diatoms are not able to reproduce fast because of insufficient light for photo-synthesis. The supply of detritus must be at its greatest in autumn and winter, because of the seasonal die-back of plants

and autumnal leaf-fall from trees, and the invertebrate bottom
fauna is usually at its richest and most varied during the winter
and spring. During summer many insects are represented only
by eggs or aerial adults, but throughout the autumn, winter
and spring their nymphs and larvae are active and grow.
Many molluscs breed in spring and early summer and may have
lifespans of only one year so that the adults die after breeding
and only small specimens are present in early summer. Crustaceans such as shrimps and slaters, however, multiply in summer
and supply a source of fish food then, as do the water fleas of the
plankton, littoral and weeds (see Table 10).

Fish such as trout feed all the year round. McCormack
(1962) has recently recorded trout with full stomachs in a small

TABLE 22. RELATION BETWEEN FAT STORAGE, AS SHOWN BY THE
COEFFICIENT OF CONDITION, AND SURVIVAL OF CARP FINGERLINGS
FROM THE R. AMUR (KIRPICHNIKOV, 1958, FROM NIKOLSKY, 1961)

Average coefficient of condition*	Time of survival at 0°C (in days)
1·92	6
2·29	10
2·33	15
2·40–2·50	over 40

$$* \text{ Coefficient of condition} = \frac{100 \times \text{weight (g)}}{\text{length (cm)}^3}$$

beck in winter where the temperature was fluctuating daily
between 0° and $3\frac{1}{2}$°C; Campbell (1963) found trout feeding in
Loch Garry at similar temperatures.

Some of our fishes show a winter fast. This is well marked in
the case of bream and silver bream. Roach probably also fast
for a while in the winter and rudd feed little at this time of
year. Fish which undergo a winter fast must lay down stores
of fat during the summer and slowly consume these in winter
to maintain the basal metabolism; their survival depends very
much on the amount of fat stored, as illustrated by data for
carp (Table 22). The coefficient of condition is an indication
of the fatness of the fish.

Nikolsky (1961) points out that "overwintering", which he
defines as "a reduced activity, complete cessation or sharp

reduction of the consumption of food, and a fall in the level of metabolism and its maintenance at the expense of energy resources accumulated in the organism, particularly fat deposits", is most widely distributed among fish of temperate fresh waters. Arctic fishes usually feed all the year round and may even increase activity in winter; crucian carp and the blackfish (*Dallia*) are exceptions, for they dig themselves into the mud of lakes and may even be frozen there.

Many still-water fishes of temperate latitudes are less active in winter and either congregate in deep water or move into streams. Nikolsky sees this as a device to avoid death from de-oxygenation in stagnant water covered by ice, but when plant-eating fishes of running water overwinter he considers this an adaptation to the absence of food-plants. Nikolsky quotes the carp and grass-carp (*Ctenopharyngodon*) as species which overwinter in the northern areas of their distribution but not in southern areas, where they continue to feed almost as actively through the winter as during the summer. Perhaps the widespread deaths of carp in Britain during the severe winter of 1962/63 were either because the fish had not stored up enough fat for successful overwintering or else because they were of a stock which has no "tradition" of overwintering.

Overwintering is quite uncommon among fish living in rivers and Hartley found no indication of a winter fast in dace, gudgeon, perch, ruffe and pike, although all these fed less actively in winter than in summer.

To sum up, where the water is turbulent and there are few rooted plants, there may be many invertebrate animals and the fish are characteristically carnivorous or piscivorous; where the water is stagnant, with a muddy bottom and many plants, the invertebrate animals either burrow in the mud or form a dense plankton among the plants, and the fishes are mostly omnivorous and able to suck up the bottom mud or masticate plant material. Between these extremes are mixed communities of carnivores and omnivores; each fish species specializes to some extent but there is much overlap in diet and all can change their food to a greater or lesser extent.

A community of fishes with a variety of feeding habits needs an environment with a properly balanced flora and fauna and a variety of ecological niches. Human activities can interfere with the balanced conditions of natural waters in various ways. The dredging and canalization of rivers imposes uniformity and thus impoverishes the environment and results in poorer angling. The creation of reservoirs is usually followed by "regulation" of the water level, and the fluctuations of this reduce the littoral fauna and thus depress the growth rates of fish such as trout. Heated effluents and sewage effluents, however well treated they may be, increase the productivity of a water, encouraging plant growth and tending to produce muddy deposits; anglers then find that trout fishing deteriorates but fishing for bream may well improve.

Chapter 6

Commercial aspects of freshwater fishes

Francis Buckland was very interested in the edibility of animals and in their exploitation as human food, so it is appropriate that I should now consider our freshwater fishes from this point of view. As a nation, we do not take them very seriously, perhaps because we traditionally have an abundant and varied supply of marine fishes. The fact that freshwater fishes present a source of first-class protein (Table 23) which

TABLE 23. THE PERCENTAGE COMPOSITION OF VARIOUS FISHES AND OTHER FOODS (NORMAN 1931, REVISED BY GREENWOOD 1963)

	Water	Protein	Fats	Fuel value as Cals per lb
Herring (average)	72·5	19·5	7·1	660
Mackerel	73·4	18·7	7·1	645
Halibut	75·4	18·6	5·2	565
Cod	82·6	16·5	0·4	325
Salmon	61·4	17·5	17·8	1080
Silver eel	53·7	13·4	32·9	1635
Yellow eel	71·2	17·6	7·9	660
Brown trout	80·5	18·0	0·7	365
Perch	78·8	18·5	1·4	402
Pike	79·5	18·8	0·7	377
Carp	78·9	15·8	4·8	495
Bream	78·7	16·2	4·1	473
Chicken	63·7	19·3	16·3	1045
Loin of beef	61·3	19·0	19·1	1155
Leg of mutton	67·4	19·8	12·4	890

could be easily tapped is not enough, since housewives must be willing to buy the fishes and to prepare them for their families, so problems of palatability and ease of preparation are also involved. I have eaten many of our species, perhaps not always prepared in the most suitable (though usually elaborate) manner, and I must confess that I did not find the cyprinids palatable. Most people enjoy salmon and trout; char and whitefish are locally highly esteemed; perch, in my opinion, are very good and so are pike if they are not too large (up to 8 to 10 lb) but it is necessary to know the position of the hooked intermuscular bones; eels are excellent eating, both fresh and smoked. I have never tasted grayling but they are said to have a delicate flavour. The rest, I think, need very special treatment to make them palatable, for even when eaten in countries where they are highly esteemed locally, fish such as carp seem to me to taste of little except the excellent sauce served with them.

Commercial fisheries may either exploit a natural population or depend on artificial propagation and rearing of fishes in ponds. At present, we exploit natural populations of salmon, sea-trout, and eels and there are small local fisheries for some of our whitefishes and char. The latter are now mainly spare-time occupations for boatmen or other local residents. The migratory fishes are conveniently caught as they are moving upstream or downstream preparatory to spawning, and at this stage they are in prime condition.

Most commercial fisheries for salmon and sea-trout are in estuaries, and the Bledisloe Committee comment in their Report (1961): "the outstanding feature of the methods of commercial fishing is their primitive nature". The Report gives annual catches of salmon and sea-trout for the 23 principal rivers in England and Wales up to 1959; some of the figures start in the 1860s. Approximate totals for salmon for the last three years of these records are:

Number of salmon caught

	By rods	*By nets (and engines)*	*Totals*
1957	15,000	28,500	43,500
1958	18,000	25,500	43,500
1959	12,750	27,750	40,500

Many of the rod-caught salmon are sent to Billingsgate Market or sold locally, so the annual value of the salmon harvest is quite large. The numbers caught in Scotland are much larger – 205,000 salmon weighing over $1\frac{1}{2}$ million lb were landed in 1962. About two thousand tons of salmon were landed in the whole of the British Isles in 1963.

Government-sponsored research on salmon is proceeding in England, Ireland and Scotland with the aim of improving the stocks while encouraging the maximum possible catches, and various people have expressed the hope that rivers such as the Thames, which used to hold salmon but lost their stocks because of pollution, will eventually be cleaned up sufficiently to hold salmon again. Sea-trout are much smaller fish, on average, but the annual catches in some rivers run into thousands and all these fish are edible. The landings in Scotland in 1962 were 275,000 sea-trout with an average weight of 2 lb.

There are two stages in their life histories when eels migrate in large numbers. The first is when the small elvers (glass eels) move up the rivers after their drift across the Atlantic Ocean and metamorphosis from leptocephalus larvae at the edge of the continental shelf. This movement is in April or May and is most spectacular in our western rivers. It is famous in the Severn, where masses of the small, wriggling fishes are scooped out with nets, cooked and compressed into small cakes called "eel-fare" which are much appreciated locally; some people eat the elvers uncooked or fried like whitebait. The second migration is the downstream movement of silver eels after they have spent three to twenty years feeding in fresh waters. These eels move downstream in late summer and autumn, usually when the water level is rising after heavy rain. The fish migrate by night when there is no moonlight, and the migration can be stopped by lights or the eels can be deflected by light barriers from the main river into sidestreams and traps. There is a controversy as to whether our eels eventually migrate across the Atlantic Ocean to spawn in the Sargasso Sea or whether all European eels are a variety of the American eel, *Anguilla rostrata*, and it is only eels from America which succeed in spawning (Tucker, 1959; Bruun, 1963). In any case, all European eels are of the same stock and the distribution of elvers is a matter of chance and the ocean currents. If Tucker is right, and all European eels are doomed to die without issue, there is no good reason why all the silver eels in Europe should not be trapped and eaten, since our supplies depend on Americans and Canadians allowing some individuals to spawn.

Even if our eels are really a separate species we could, in theory, trap all the silver eels in British rivers without much affecting future stocks – provided that the whole of Europe did not do the same but allowed some eels to proceed to sea.

In the last century, eels were appreciated as food, and almost every millstream in the south and west of England was provided with its eel-trap. At present, there is a commercial fishery in Northern Ireland, on the River Bann below Lough Neagh. The upstream movement of elvers in spring is encouraged, even to the extent of catching them near the estuary and transporting them alive and releasing them into the lough; the silver eels are trapped as they move downstream in autumn. Elsewhere in the British Isles there are a few eel-traps, but the total yield is negligible, certainly less than 100 tons from south-east England. This is a great waste of valuable food, because hundreds of thousands of eels could be caught without very great effort. The Bledisloe Report states "we import about 2000 tons of eels a year" and these could certainly be supplied from our own stocks. There is clearly already some market for eels and I believe that this could be enlarged. The fish must always be marketed alive and are relatively easy to keep, even for months, although the food value falls off since they are not fed. There is popular prejudice against them because of their snake-like appearance and sliminess. The housewife presented with a lively eel may well feel unable to cope with the business of killing and then skinning it, a process as simple as peeling off a stocking once the knack is acquired. Perhaps these common fish would be more appreciated if they were sold frozen or tinned, in competition with exotic dainties such as kangaroo tails, instead of alive in the fishmonger's tub. One of the main selling lines at present is jellied eels, and smoked eels are an expensive delicacy.

Yellow eels live in rivers, streams, ponds and lakes all over the country; where they are common, they can be captured in traps such as Dutch fyke nets. Anglers are merely exasperated when they hook eels, and these fish are certainly better removed from most fishing waters, more especially where there are trout and salmon since they compete for food with these fishes. Yellow eels are highly nutritious even though they contain less fat than silver eels. Establishing local markets and fisheries for them would benefit anglers and increase our home-produced supply of first-class protein.

Other species with natural populations which might be exploited as food are the perch and pike. Some lakes and reservoirs contain large numbers of perch which are often stunted because of over-crowding. The Freshwater Biological Association have shown on Windermere that fish can easily be trapped when they congregate to breed in the shallows in early spring. It is unnecessary even to bait the wire-netting traps, and the catch consists largely of male fishes so that many females are left to spawn again. During the war, the perch were caught intensively in Windermere and were canned and sold under the name "perchines". Observations ever since have followed the effects of the heavy fishing, which reduced the population to about one-twentieth of its pre-war numbers, on the growth of the surviving perch and their progeny. Economically, the real problem is that the actual yield of such perch fisheries would be relatively small quantities spread over many lakes and available only for a few weeks each year. Canning and freezing again seem possible ways of promoting sales.

Pike are caught in gill-nets in Windermere between October and February by the Freshwater Biological Association, who usually remove about 1 ton of pike each year. The pike caught now are mostly 3 to 6 years old and are therefore of the size when they make excellent eating (5 to 7 lb weight). The F.B.A. do not sell their catch; their fishing is undertaken for scientific reasons.

Anglers' feelings about pike are somewhat complicated; some people enjoy fishing for them, others regard them as voracious competitors. Many anglers believe that pike can be useful because they will remove sick and stunted fish of other species and thus lead to better angling. The study of the pike in Windermere has shown that, as might be expected, the size of the prey increases with the size of the pike. The largest pike eat trout, smaller ones eat perch, and those less than 12 inches long may eat minnows; pike of all sizes eat char at the time when these are spawning in the shallows in November. The larger pike eat perch and trout which are three years old and older and these are the fish desired by the anglers, so there is direct competition between man and pike. If pike are added to a water with a stunted population of perch or roach they will certainly eat these fishes, but the pike will grow fast and soon will be selecting the larger individuals instead of helping the angler by feasting on the smaller ones. In these circumstances, a fishery for pike which would remove them before they became larger than about 8 lb could be very helpful in maintaining a population of young pike, many of which would be the right size to eat the small, stunted fish. Individual fisheries would not yield heavy crops of pike but it is a pity that this potential source of delicious fish should be totally neglected.

One possible solution to this problem of small fisheries, scattered over the country and with seasonal yields, is to persuade a chain of restaurants to take up freshwater fish as a "spécialité de la maison" and to encourage their customers to eat each species when it is in season. Even so, very few people would be able to make a living from this type of fishing and I think it would always have to be a sideline or seasonal occupation.

Pond fisheries, rearing rainbow trout for the table, are likely to become an increasing feature in this country, judging from the recent surge of interest. The essentials are firstly, a good water supply with sufficient land to lay out series of ponds to make the best use of the water, and secondly, a reliable and inexpensive food supply. The water must be plentiful in summer, and ideally should be from a spring so that it is warm in winter and close to the optimum temperature throughout the year; rainbow trout are quite hardy, with a greater tolerance than brown trout. Successful pond fisheries have been run in Denmark for many years and there the trout are fed on small sea-fish which are a useless by-product of the coast fisheries. Rainbow trout grow faster than brown trout and can be raised to marketable size in a year or less, and are sold in Britain as well as in many other countries, including Switzerland. Spawning stocks are maintained from which eggs and milt are stripped, and the processes of rearing can all be controlled to give a maximum yield of marketable fish. In America, trout in hatcheries have been reared for many years on artificial diets. In the early days these needed to be supplemented by rations of fresh meat and/or liver, but modern diets are alleged to contain all the vitamins and growth substances required for rearing healthy fish. The diets come in dry pellets of various sizes suitable for fish of different lengths, and the whole business of rearing fish becomes rather like rearing poultry – doling out appropriate rations at appropriate intervals. It is all much simpler than the buying of carcases and their carving and mincing up for trout food which was the basis of hatchery practice in Britain before the war. Modern diets are very concentrated and there is a real danger of overfeeding, with resulting deaths from fatty degeneration of the liver. The other main danger of pond-rearing is the spread of epidemic diseases, especially if the fish are overcrowded, but avoiding these is a matter of taking precautions and keeping the fish under close observation so that action can be taken as soon as danger symptoms are observed.

At present there are a number of commercial hatcheries in Britain, but their business is almost entirely the supply of trout to anglers for stocking waters where natural reproduction is not sufficient to maintain adequate stocks. Some of these hatcheries also supply coarse fish and this seems to be an increasing trade. These fishes have small, delicate eggs, often sticky, and they are more difficult to rear than salmonids. The usual technique is to place adult fish in suitable ponds and allow them to spawn naturally. The adults are then removed and the young fish are reared in the ponds. Different species require different inducements to spawn – thus carp and bream will use piles of brush-wood suspended in the water, but tench must be given a more elaborate shelter. Providing suitable food for the young fry may be a difficulty, too. On the whole, it is much easier to find a water with a plentiful supply of the required species and to catch some of these by netting or electric fishing and transport them away than to rear them from the egg. It may be worth while to rear rather scarce fish, such as carp, but even these are usually imported as young fish because they prefer warmer water for spawning than is usually available at our fish farms, which were all originally designed for rearing the coldwater salmonids.

This leads me to the possibility of using the warm water from power stations and factories for producing fish for the table, and also using sewage farms as fish ponds. Since we eat only the muscles, the danger of contamination with disease through such fishes is very slight. Rainbow trout were reared in partly treated sewage effluent at Munich before the war, but these are carnivorous fishes and crop the herbivores and detritus feeders which benefit directly from the fertilizing effect of the sewage. Herbivorous fish would be more economical in trapping the energy in the sewage, and such fishes as *Tilapia* species from Africa could be grown in heated effluents. These are very good to eat, in my opinion even better than salmon and trout. Since they are warmwater stenotherms they would die if the water temperature fell below summer temperatures, so they could not spread into normal waters and interfere with our native fauna. Where there is a constant supply of heated water, their cultivation is well worth considering.

Thus there are commercial possibilities in exploiting some of our freshwater fishes as food in addition to those already used, but I feel sure that the greatest value of our fishes will always be that they provide recreation for anglers. I will therefore conclude by considering our fish fauna from their point of view.

Salmon are today limited by water pollution to rivers in the less industrial areas of the British Isles, that is, mainly to rivers in Ireland, Scotland, Wales, south-west England and the Lake District. As sport fishes, they are available only to anglers living by or able to visit these more remote waters. Traditionally, they are the most exciting fish to catch and they have a high market value as esteemed food, so the cost of salmon fishing puts it beyond the scope of the majority of British anglers.

Brown trout are very widely distributed in the British Isles and potentially are capable of living in almost all our waters – the exceptions are where the oxygen content in summer always falls below about 5 cc/l. There are many waters where trout can survive and grow but are unable to spawn, and here there must be regular stocking to supply trout for the angler. Trout can maintain populations in competition with coarse fishes where there is a current of 25 cm/sec or faster, or plenty of oxygen, but they do not compete successfully where the water is still and the oxygen concentration rather low – there are thus a great many places where trout could be maintained if coarse fishes were excluded, but good trout fishing is unlikely if these, especially roach, are present. South-country reservoirs, such as Chew Valley Lake, and gravel pits are examples of such waters.

The term "coarse fishes" includes many species, each with preferred habitats, but most of them do well in water with little or no current where plants flourish. Here there are mixed communities, the exact balance between species depending on depth, flow, amount of weed and so on. Traditionally, trout fishing is a more expensive business than coarse fishing, and usually it is better managed in the sense that more care and money are spent on developing the fishing. Because of the greater tolerance of coarse fishes, this fishing is usually available near industrial centres where it would be difficult (and expensive) to maintain stocks of trout. The effects of industrialization on rivers is to tip the balance in favour of coarse fishes by increasing the productivity of the water and often by warming it up.

Close seasons are imposed to protect breeding fish, so for salmonids the close season will be in autumn and winter, and for coarse fishes in early summer. I am not going to discuss whether such seasons are properly applied or strictly necessary, but they do give a respite from fishing during which work can be undertaken on the water without interfering with sport, and they may be worth while just for this. Salmonids are not good to eat when just spent, so the close season means that these tasteless fish are not caught. For anyone who wishes to fish all through the year, the answer seems to be to angle for trout and for coarse fishes, each at the appropriate time, and to press for both types of fishing to be made available locally.

Both types of angling require considerable skill for success and therefore both can be a continuing interest. To fish with good results for almost any species entails some knowledge of its natural history and requires keen observation of the changing weather and water conditions. I think it is an excellent thing that this sport is claiming an ever-widening circle of participants and I wish for each one with Izaak Walton "that if he be an honest Angler, the east wind may never blow when he goes a-fishing".

Bibliography

General books on fishes and fresh waters

DAY, F. (1880–4). *The Fishes of Great Britain and Ireland*, Vols. 1 & 2. London, Williams and Norgate. Vol. 1: 336 pp. Vol. 2: 388 pp.

HYNES, H. B. N. (1960). *The Biology of Polluted Waters*. Liverpool. 202 pp.

JENKINS, J. T. (1936). *The Fishes of the British Isles, both Freshwater and Salt*. London, Frederick Warne and Co. 408 pp.

MAGRI MacMAHON, A. F. (1946). *Fishlore*. Pelican Books. 208 pp.

NIKOLSKY, G. V. (1961). (translated by L. Birkett, 1963). *The Ecology of Fishes*. New York, Academic Press Inc. 352 pp.

NORMAN, J. R. (1931). (revised by P. H. Greenwood, 1963). *A History of Fishes*. London, Benn. 398 pp.

REGAN, C. T. (1911). *The Freshwater Fishes of the British Isles*. London, Methuen and Co. Ltd. 287 pp.

SCHINDLER, O. (1953). (translated by P. A. Orkin, 1957). *Freshwater Fishes*. London, Thames and Hudson. 243 pp.

WALTON, IZAAK. (1653). *The Compleat Angler*.

References quoted in the text

ALABASTER, J. S. (1963). The effect of heated effluents on fish. *Int. J. Air Wat. Pollut.*, **7**, 541–563.

ALM, G. (1959). Connection between maturity, size and age in fishes. *Rep. Inst. Freshwat. Res. Drottningholm*, No. 40, 5–145.

AUDIGÉ, P. (1921). Sur la croissance des poissons maintenus en milieu de température constante. *C. r. Séanc. Soc. Biol.*, **172**, 287–9.

BAGGERMAN, B. (1957). An experimental study on the timing of breeding and migration in the three-spined stickleback (*Gasterosteus aculeatus* L.). *Archs neerl. Zool.*, **12**, 105–317.

BISHAI, H. M. (1960a). The effect of gas content of water on larval and young fish. *Z. wiss. Zool.*, **163**, 37–64.

BISHAI, H. M. (1960b). Upper lethal temperatures for larval salmonids. *J. Cons. perm. int. Explor. Mer*, **25**, 129–133.

BLEDISLOE COMMITTEE (1961). Report of committee on Salmon and Freshwater Fisheries. Cmnd. 1350, HMSO, London. 151 pp.

BRETT, J. R. (1956). Some principles in the thermal requirements of fishes. *Q. Rev. Biol.*, **31**, 75–87.

BROWN, M. E. (1946a). The growth of brown trout (*Salmo trutta* Linn.). I. Factors influencing the growth of trout fry. *J. exp. Biol.*, **22**, 118–129.

BROWN, M. E. (1946b). The growth of brown trout (*Salmo trutta* Linn.). II. The growth of two-year-old trout at a constant temperature of 11·5°C. *J. exp. Biol.*, **22**, 130–144.

BROWN, M. E. (1946c). The growth of brown trout (*Salmo trutta* Linn.). III. The effect of temperature on the growth of two-year-old trout. *J. exp. Biol.*, **22**, 145–155.

BROWN, M. E. (1951). The growth of brown trout (*Salmo trutta* Linn.). IV. The effect of food and temperature on the survival and growth of fry. *J. exp. Biol.*, **28**, 473–491.

BRUUN, A. F. (1963). The breeding of the North Atlantic freshwater-eels. *Adv. mar. Biol.*, **1**, 137–169.

BULLOUGH, W. S. (1939). A study of the reproductive cycle of the minnow in relation to the environment. *Proc. zool. Soc. Lond.*, A, **109**, 79–102.

BULLOUGH, W. S. (1940). The effect of the reduction of light in spring on the breeding season of the minnow (*Phoxinus laevis* Linn.). *Proc. zool. Soc. Lond.*, A, **110**, 149–157.

CAMPBELL, R. N. (1963). Some effects of impoundment on the environment and growth of brown trout (*Salmo trutta* L.) in Loch Garry (Inverness-shire). *Freshwat. Salm. Fish. Res.*, No. 30, 27 pp.

CARPENTER, K. E. (1928). *Life in Inland Waters with Especial Reference to Animals.* London, Sidgwick and Jackson Ltd., 267 pp.

COCKING, A. W. (1959a). The effects of high temperatures on roach (*Rutilus rutilus*). I. The effects of constant high temperatures. *J. exp. Biol.*, **36**, 203–216.

COCKING, A. W. (1959b). The effects of high temperatures on roach (*Rutilus rutilus*). II. The effects of temperature increasing at a known constant rate. *J. exp. Biol.*, **36**, 217–226.

COLMAN, J. S. (1950). *The Sea and its Mysteries.* London, G. Bell and Sons Ltd. 285 pp.

DOWNING, K. M. and MERKENS, J. C. (1957). The influence of temperature on the survival of several species of fish in low tensions of dissolved oxygen. *Ann. appl. Biol.*, **45**, 261–7.

ELTON, C. (1927). *Animal Ecology.* London, Sidgwick and Jackson Ltd. 207 pp.

FROST, W. E. and BROWN, M. E. (1967). *The Trout.* Collins, London.

FRY, F. E. J. (1957). *The Physiology of Fishes*, **1**, 1–63 (Ed. M. E. Brown). The aquatic respiration of fish. New York, Academic Press Inc. 447 pp.

FRY, F. E. J., BRETT, J. R. and CLAWSON, G. H. (1942). Lethal limits of temperature for young goldfish. *Rev. Can. Biol.*, **1**, 50–56.

FRY, F. E. J., HART, J. S. and WALKER, K. F. (1946). Lethal temperature relations for a sample of young speckled trout, *Salvelinus fontinalis*. *Univ. Toronto Stud. biol. Ser.*, No. 54, 9–35.

GIBSON, E. S. (1951). Ph.D. Thesis, University of Toronto.

HARTLEY, P. H. T. (1947). The natural history of some British freshwater fishes. *Proc. zool. Soc. Lond.*, **117**, 129–206.

HARTLEY, P. H. T. (1948). Food and feeding relationships in a community of freshwater fishes. *J. Anim. Ecol.*, **17**, 1–14.

HAZARD, T. P. and EDDY, R. E. (1951). Modification of the sexual cycle in brook trout (*Salvelinus fontinalis*) by control of light. *Trans. Am. Fish. Soc.*, **80**, 158–162.

HICKEY, M. D. and HARRIS, J. R. (1947). Progress of the *Diphyllobothrium* Epizootic at Poulaphouca Reservoir, County Wicklow, Ireland. *J. Helminth.*, **22**, 12–28.

HOLMES, P. F. (1960). The brown trout of Malham Tarn, Yorkshire. *Salm. Trout Mag.*, **159**, 127–145.

HUET, M. (1949). Aperçu des relations entre la pente et les populations piscicoles des eaux courantes. *Schweiz. Z. Hydrol.*, **11**, 332–351.

HUET, M. (1954). Biologie, profils en long et en travers des eaux courantes. *Bull. fr. Piscic.*, **175**, 41–53.

HUET, M. (1962). Influence du courant sur la distribution des poissons dans les eaux courantes. *Schweiz. Z. Hydrol.*, **24**, 412–432.

HYNES, H. B. N. (1963). Imported organic matter and secondary productivity in streams. *Int. Congr. Zool.*, *Washington*, **4**, 324–329.

KALLEBERG, H. (1958). Observations in a stream tank of territoriality and competition in juvenile salmon and trout (*Salmo salar* L. and *S. trutta* L.). *Rep. Inst. Freshwat. Res. Drottningholm*, No. 39, 55–98.

142   Bibliography

KEMPE, O. (1962). The growth of the roach (*Leuciscus rutilus* L.) in some Swedish lakes. *Rep. Inst. Freshwat. Res. Drottningholm*, No. 44, 42–104.

KREITMANN, L. (1932). Contributions à l'étude des characteristiques des passes a poissons. La vitesse de nage des poissons. *Verh. Int. Verein. theoret. limnol.*, 5, 345–53.

LE CREN, E. D. (1958). Observations on the growth of perch (*Perca fluviatilis*) over twenty-two years with special reference to the effects of temperature and changes in population density. *J. Anim. Ecol.*, 27, 287–334.

LE CREN, E. D. (1961). How many fish survive? *River Bds. Ass. Yb.*, 9, 57–64.

MACAN, T. T. (1958). The temperature of a small stony stream. *Hydrobiologia*, 12, 89–106.

MAGRI MACMAHON, A. F. (1946). *Fishlore*. Pelican Books. 208 pp.

MANLEY, G. (1936). The climate of the Northern Pennines: the coldest part of England. *Q. Jl R. met. Soc.*, 62, 103–113.

McCORMACK, J. C. (1962). The food of young trout (*Salmo trutta*) in two different becks. *J. Anim. Ecol.*, 31, 305–316.

MONTÈN, E. (1948). Undersökningar över gäddynglets biologi och några därmed samman-hangande problem. *Skr. söd. Sver. Fiskför.*, 1948, Nr. 1.

NIKOLSKY, G. V. (1961). (translated by L. Birkett, 1963). *The Ecology of Fishes*. New York, Academic Press Inc. 352 pp.

NORMAN, J. R. (1931). (revised by P. H. Greenwood, 1963). *A History of Fishes*. London, Benn. 398 pp.

PERCIVAL, E. and WHITEHEAD, H. (1929). A quantitative study of the fauna of some types of stream-bed. *J. Ecol.*, 17, 282–314.

REGAN, C. T. (1911). *The Freshwater Fishes of the British Isles*. London, Methuen and Co. Ltd. 287 pp.

SCHINDLER, O. (1953). (translated by P. A. Orkin, 1957). *Freshwater Fishes*. London, Thames and Hudson. 243 pp.

SLACK, H. D., et al. (1957). *Studies on Loch Lomond*. I. Glasgow; Blackie and Son Ltd., for Univ. Glasgow. 133 pp.

SMYLY, W. J. P. (1952). Observations on the food of the fry of perch (*Perca fluviatilis* Linn.) in Windermere. *Proc. zool. Soc. Lond.*, 122, 407–416.·

SWIFT, D. R. (1961). The annual growth-rate cycle in brown trout (*Salmo trutta* Linn.) and its cause. *J. exp. Biol.*, 38, 595–604.

SWIFT, D. R. (1964). The effect of temperature and oxygen on the growth rate of the Windermere char (*Salvelinus alpinus Willughbii*). *Comp. Biochems Physiol.*, 12, 179–183.

SWIFT, D. R. (1965a). Effect of temperature on mortality and rate of development of the eggs of the Windermere char (*Salvelinus alpinus*). *J. Fish. Res. Bd. Canada*, 22, 913–917.

SWIFT, D. R. (1965b). Effect of temperature on mortality and rate of development of the eggs of the pike (*Esox lucius*) and the perch (*Perca fluviatilis* L.). *Nature Lond.*, 206, 528.

TANSLEY, A. G. (1939). *The British Islands and their Vegetation*. Cambridge.

TORBETT, H. (1961). *The Angler's Freshwater Fishes*. London.

TUCKER, D. W. (1959). A new solution to the Atlantic eel problem. *Nature, Lond.*, 183, 495–501.

WALTON, IZAAK. (1653). *The Compleat Angler*.

WEATHERLEY, A. H. (1963). Zoogeography of *Perca fluviatilis* (Linnaeus) and *Perca flavescens* (Mitchill) with special reference to the effects of high temperature. *Proc. zool. Soc. Lond.*, 141, 557–576.

WINGFIELD, C. A. (1940). The effect of certain environmental factors on the growth of brown trout (*Salmo trutta* L.). *J. exp. Biol.*, 17, 435–448.

WORTHINGTON, E. B. (1940). Rainbows. A report on attempts to acclimatize rainbow trout in Britain. *Salm. Trout Mag.*, **100**, 241–60.

WORTHINGTON, E. B. (1941). Rainbows. A report on attempts to acclimatize rainbow trout in Britain. (Continued). *Salm. Trout Mag.*, **101**, 62–99.

WUNDER, W. (1936). Physiologie der Süsswasser-fische Mitteleuropas. *Handb. Binnenfisch. Mitteleur.*, 2B.

INDEX

Age, at death, 107–9
at maturity, 93–4, 101–6
Angling, 13–14, 25–8, 52, 130, 138–9

Barbel, *Barbus barbus*, 16, 26, 49–50, 53–4, 56–8, 85, 89, 95
Bass, Large-mouth, *Micropterus salmoides*, 26
Small-mouth, *M. dolomieui*, 26
Behaviour, feeding, 114–19, 121–6
of fry, 98–100, 109, 119, 121, 125–6
spawning, 92–3, 95, 97–8, 105–6
and temperature, 30, 33–6, 41, 43, 47
territorial, 98–100, 125–6
Bitterling, *Rhodeus amarus*, 16, 19, 26
Blackfish, *Dallia*, 129
Bleak, *Alburnus alburnus*, 16, 26, 35, 54, 58, 89, 90
Bream, Common, *Abramis brama*, 26, 28, 33, 35, 37, 44, 46, 49, 52, 54, 56–8, 61–2, 85, 88–90, 94–5, 97–8, 101–2, 107, 117–19, 121–3, 126–7, 130–1
Silver or White, *Blicca bjoernka*, 16, 25, 54, 56, 89, 122–3
Bullhead or Miller's Thumb, *Cottus gobio*, 15–16, 26, 46, 50, 53–5, 58, 89, 95, 98, 113, 119–20, 127
Burbot, *Lota lota*, 15–16, 25, 46, 89, 96

Carp, Common *Cyprinus carpio*, 16, 25, 27, 31, 33–4, 37, 43–4, 46, 50–2, 54, 57–8, 61, 89, 95–7, 100, 102, 107, 117–18, 127–9, 131–2
Crucian, *Carassius carassius*, 16, 33, 45–6, 85, 129
Grass, *Ctenopharyngodon idella*, 26, 129
Catfish, see Wels
Char, *Salvelinus alpinus*, 16, 20, 22, 25, 31, 42, 43, 50, 61–2, 89, 95–6, 102, 126–7, 132, 135
Chub, *Squalius cephalus*, 16, 25–6, 37, 44–6, 49, 52, 54, 56–8, 85, 89, 95, 102, 117
Climate, 19–21, 87, and see Temperature, Seasonal changes

Competition, 27–8, 98–9, 109, 121–2, 125–6
Crustaceans (shrimps, slaters, water fleas), 59–62, 88, 90, 112–13, 115, 119–128
Current, 53–60, 62–3, 97–8

Dace, *Leuciscus leuciscus*, 16, 26, 28, 54, 57, 85, 91, 102, 113, 117, 119–21, 129
Daylength, 87–97
Death, see Age, Mortality
Detritus, 59, 64, 87, 112–13, 116, 118–19, 127–8
Distribution, natural, 21–6
by man, 25–8

Economic value of fish, as food, 13, 131–8
for sport, 13, 138–9
Eel, Yellow and Silver, *Anguilla anguilla*, 13, 15–16, 23–4, 54, 58–9, 94, 113, 119–21, 127, 131–4
Effluents, 39, 52, 63, 86, 130, and see Pollution
Eggs (ova), *Plates 15, 17;* 85, 95–8, 110
numbers of, 96–7, 104, 108–9
rate of development of, 49–51, 95, 97, 109
sizes of, 49–51, 95–7, 104
survival of, 49–51, 100, 104, 109
temperature tolerance of, 49–51, 108
European fauna, 19, 21, 27

Flounder, *Platichthys (Pleuronectes) flesus*, 15–16
Food, see also Metabolism
of adult fish, 90, 111–130
conversion into fish flesh, 113–14
of fry, 95, 97–100, 109–10, 119, 121, 125–6
requirements, 30, 35, 43–4, 113
seasonal changes in, 88, 90, 127–9
variation from place to place, 59–62, 85, 123
webs, 111–14

Fry (0 + fish), behaviour of, 97–100, 109–10
  food of, 95, 97, 110, 119, 121, 123, 125–6
  mortality (survival) of, 98–101, 108
  temperature tolerance of, 33, 51

Goldfish, *Carassius auratus*, 16, 30–4, 37, 44–5
Gradient, 53–7, 60
Grayling, *Thymallus thymallus*, 16, 26, 32–3, 35, 37, 46, 49–50, 52, 64, 56–7, 89, 95–6, 102, 132
Grey Mullet, *Mugil* spp., 15–16
Growth, and diet, 90, 123–7
  and maturity, 101–5, 108, 113
  and season, 89–91
  and temperature, 30, 35–42, 88–91, 101, 123
Gudgeon, *Gobio gobio*, 16, 33, 35, 46, 54, 89, 95, 101–2, 113, 119–21, 126, 129

Hormones, 44, 92–4
Houting, *Coregonus oxyrhynchus*, 21–2
Huchen, *Hucho hucho*, 28

Ice, 19–21, 23–5, 29, 43, 64
Ide or Orfe, *Idus idus*, 16, 19
Insects, aquatic, 59–62, 88, 90, 100, 112–13, 115, 119–28
  terrestrial, 88, 90
Invertebrate aquatic animals, 59–62, 64, 88–9, 112–30

Lakes and still waters, 21–2, 26–8, 39–42, 52, 60–64, 85, 126–7, 129–30
  Blagdon reservoir, 27, 60
  Blenheim Lake, *Plate 11*
  Chew Valley Reservoir, 60, 139
  Ennerdale Water, 60
  Lake Mälären, 90–1, 123
  Lake Sarnasjön, 123
  Loch Choin, 100
  Loch Garry, 89
  Loch Lomond, 41, 60, 100–1
  Loch Rannoch, *Plate 9*
  Loch Tummel, *Plate 10*
  Lochan an Daim, *Plate 12*
  Lough Derg, 60, 119

Lakes and still waters—*continued*
  Lough Neagh, 134
  Malham Tarn, 60, 107
  Norfolk Broads, 26, 60, 123–4
  Wastwater, 60
  Weir Wood Reservoir, 60
  Windermere, 60, 89–90, 107, 135
  Woburn pond, 26
Lampreys (Cyclostomata), 16, 25
Length, see Size
Loach, Spiny, *Cobitis taenia*, 16
  Stone, *Nemacheilus barbatulus*, 16, 46, 54, 58, 89, 95, 101–2, 107, 113, 119, 121, 126

Maturity, 93–4, 101–7
Metabolism, 29–30, 35–6, 44–9, 90, 111–12, 129
Migratory fishes, 21, 24–5, 27, 85, 92–4, 108, 133–4
Miller's Thumb, see Bullhead
Minnow, *Phoxinus phoxinus*, 16, 28, 37, 44, 46, 49, 50, 53–8, 62, 85, 89, 94–5, 100–2, 106–7, 113, 119–21, 126–7, 135
Molluscs (limpets, mussels, snails), 59–62, 88, 112, 115, 119–28
Mortality (and Survival), 43–4, 99–101, 104–110, 129

Orfe, see Ide
Overwintering, 30, 43–4, 128–9
Oxygen, 40, 43, 45–52, 110
  and activity, 46
  in different waters, 40, 52, 59–64, 85
  and eggs, 49–50, 97
  and fry, 51, 97

Parasites, 27, 107–8, 114
Perch, *Perca fluviatilis*, 15–16, 25–6, 33, 37, 43–7, 49–50, 52, 54, 58, 61, 64, 88–90, 95–6, 100, 102, 104–7, 118–19, 121, 123, 125–7, 129, 131, 135–6, *Plates 17, 18, 21, 22*
Pike, *Esox lucius*, 16, 25–6, 33, 37, 46, 49–51, 54, 58, 61, 64, 89, 95–6, 98, 100, 102, 106–7, 113–15, 119–21, 126–7, 129, 131–2, 135–6; *Plates 20, 21*

Pikeperch, *Lucioperca lucioperca,* 16, 26

Plants, aquatic flowering plants (weeds), 43, 46, 53, 55, 57–62, 85–9, 90, 95, 97, 109–16, 119–30

   phytoplankton (microscopic plants, diatoms), 61–2, 64, 97, 119, 122–4, 126

Pollution, 46, 52, and see Effluents

Powan, *Coregonus* sp., 41, 49, 50, 100–1

Rainfall, 87

Rivers and flowing waters and canals, 19, 21, 23–8, 35, 38–9, 41, 52–60, 63, 85–6, 126, 129–30

   fish zones in, 35, 53–60

   Afon Elan, *Plate 2*

   Great Ouse River, 26, 39; *Plate 7*

   Old West River, 122–4

   R. Bann, 134

   R. Blackwater (Cork), 26

   R. Cam, 26, 91, 113, 119–22, 124, 126

   R. Coln, *Plate 4*

   R. Derwent (Derbyshire), 57

   R. Erne, 26

   R. Mole, 91

   Reach Lode, 122

   R. Severn, 133

   R. Shannon, 26

   R. Tees, 41

   R. Test, 38–9

   R. Thames, 19, 23, 25 28, 91, 107, 133; *Plate 6*

   R. Trent, 25, 39; *Plate 8*

   R. Wye (Derbyshire), 27

   R. Wye (Radnorshire), *Plate 3*

   R. Yarty, *Plate 5*

   Shepreth Brook, 119–21

   Willow Brook, 91

Roach, *Rutilus rutilus,* 16, 26, 31–3, 46–7, 54, 58, 61, 85, 88–91, 94–5, 100–2, 104, 106–7, 116–21, 123–7, 136; *Plate 19*

Rudd, *Scardinius erythrophthalmus,* 16, 26, 33, 37, 54, 58, 61, 89–90, 95, 117, 126, 128

Ruffe, *Acerina cernua,* 15–16, 26, 33, 46, 50, 89, 95, 102, 118, 123, 129

Salmon, Atlantic, *Salmo salar,* 13, 16, 20, 26, 28, 33, 49–51, 53–5, 57, 89, 95–8, 102, 106–7, 114, 116, 126, 131–4

   Humpback or Pink, *Oncorhynchus gorbuscha,* 28, 32

Seasonal changes, in daylight, 87–9

   in food, 88, 90, 127–9

   in growth, 88–91

   in invertebrates and plants, 88–9, 127–8

   in temperature, 38–41, 87–95

Shad, *Alosa,* spp. 15–16

Size (Length and Weight), 93, 101–7, and see Growth

Spawning, and see Maturity

   behaviour, 92–3, 95, 97–8, 105–6

   grounds, 85, 95, 97–8, 109

   times, 37, 89, 91–8

Sterlet, *Acipenser ruthenus,* 15–16

Stickleback, Three-spined, *Gasterosteus aculeatus,* 15–16, 50, 89, 91–5, 98, 101–2, 107, 113, 119–21, 127

   Ten-spined, *Pygosteus pungitius,* 16

Stoneloach, see Loach

Sturgeon, *Acipenser sturio,* 15–16, 25, 101–2

Substratum (gravel, mud, sand), 53–5, 57–62, 85, 87–8

   and invertebrates and plants, 59–62, 126–7, 129

   and spawning, 95, 97–8, 109–10

Survival, see Mortality

Teeth, pharyngeal, 115–17, 123, 125

Temperature, 20, 29–52, 62–4, 87–95, 110, 112

   and growth, 30, 35–42, 88–91, 101, 123

   of lakes, 39–43, 63–4, 85

   lethal limits for adult fish, 30–4, 37, 42–3

   lethal limits for eggs and fry, 33, 49–51, 108

   and respiration, 30, 46–52

   of rivers, 35, 38–9, 41, 60, 62–3

   and spawning, 37, 49, 94–7

Territories, see Behaviour, territorial

Tench, *Tinca tinca,* 16, 26, 28, 33–4, 37, 46–7, 4 –50, 52, 54, 61, 85, 89, 95–6, 102, 117–18, 127

Tilapia, 138

Trout, Brown and Sea, *Salmo trutta*, 13–14, 16, 20, 24–8, 31–7, 42, 46, 48–51, 53–8, 61–2, 64, 85, 88–90, 95–108, 114–15, 119–22, 126–7, 131–2, 134–9; *Plates 13, 14, 15, 16, 20, 21, 22*
Rainbow, *Salmo gairdneri*, 16, 27–8, 33, 44–7, 115, 136, 138; *Plate 19*
Speckled (American Brook Trout), *Salvelinus fontinalis*, 16, 28, 31, 33–4, 37, 42, 44–5, 48–9, 91–2; *Plate 22*

Weight, see Size
Wels or Catfish, *Siluris glanis*, 16, 19, 26–7
Whitefishes (Gwyniad, Houting, Pollan, Powan, Schelly, Vendace), *Coregonus* spp., 16, 20, 22, 41, 43, 49–50, 61, 89, 95, 100–102, 132

Zooplankton (rotifers and water fleas), 61–2, 88, 90, 97, 100, 119, 123, 125–7, 129